Contested Legacies

Socialist History 20

Rivers Oram Press
London, Sydney and New York

Editorial Team
Kevin Morgan
Stephen Woodhams
Willie Thompson
David Parker
Mike Waite
David Morgan
Heather Williams
Julie Johnson

Editorial Advisors
Noreen Branson
Rodney Hilton
Eric Hobsbawm
David Howell
Monty Johnstone
Victor Kiernan
David Marquand
Ben Pimlott
Pat Thane

All editorial enquiries to Kevin Morgan, Department of Government, University of Manchester M13 9PL or Kevin.Morgan@man.ac.uk. Reviews enquiries to Stephen Woodhams at SWood18045@aol.com

Published in 2001
by Rivers Oram Press, an imprint of Rivers Oram Publishers Ltd
144 Hemingford Road, London N1 1DE

Distributed in the USA by
New York University Press, 838 Broadway, New York, NY 10003–4183

Distributed in Australia and New Zealand by
UNIReps, University of New South Wales, Sydney, NSW 2052

Set in Garamond by NJ Design Associates
and printed in Great Britain by T.J. International Ltd, Padstow

This edition copyright © 2001 Socialist History Society
The articles are copyright © 2001 Mark Bevir, Martin Durham, Michael Murphy, Matt Perry, David Renton, Duncan Thompson

No part of this journal may be produced in any form, except for the quotation of brief passages in criticism, without the written permission of the publishers
The right of the contributors to be identified as the authors has been asserted by them in accordance with the Copyright, Designs and Patents Act 1988

British Library Cataloguing in Publication Data
A catalogue record for this publication is available from the British Library
ISBN 1 85489 134 0 (hb)
ISBN 1 85489 135 9 (pb)
ISSN 0969 4331

Contents

Notes on Contributors	v
Editorial	vi
Socialism, Civil Society and the State in Modern Britain Mark Bevir	1
Pessimism of the Intellect? New Left Review and the 'conjuncture of 1989' Duncan Thompson	19
The Jarrow Crusade, the National Hunger March and the Labour Party in 1936 A re-appraisal Matt Perry	40
George Garrett and the Collective Memory of War Michael Murphy	54
Women and Fascism A critique David Renton	71
Fascism, Socialism and the Politics of Gender A reply Martin Durham	83

Reviews 92

Books to be remembered (3)
Bert Birtles, *Exiles in the Aegean. A personal narrative of Greek politics and travel* (John Saville) 92

E. P. Thompson, *Collected Poems* (Andy Croft) 95

Randall Swingler, *Selected Poems* (Charles Hobday) 98

Tony Shaw, *British Cinema and the Cold War. The State, Propaganda and Consensus* (Richard Taylor) 100

Geoff Andrews, Hilda Kean and Jane Thompson (eds), *Ruskin College. Contesting Knowledge, Dissenting Politics* (Bert Ward) 103

June Purvis and Sandra Stanley Holton (eds), *Votes for Women* (Cheryl Law) 105

Roderick Stackelberg, *Hitler's Germany. Origins, Interpretations, Legacies* (Louise Willmot) 109

Gerwin Strobl, *The Germanic Isle. Nazi Perceptions of Britain* (Mathew Stibbe) 111

Patrick Pasture and John Verberckmoes (eds), *Working-Class Internationalism and the Appeal of National Identity. Historical Debates and Current Perspectives on Western Europe* (Zafar Khan) 114

Raphael Samuel, *Island Stories. Unravelling Britain. Theatres of Memory, volume II* (Stephen Woodhams) 116

Notes on Contributors

Mark Bevir is a member of the department of political science at the University of California, Berkeley. His recent publications include *The Logic of the History of Ideas* (Cambridge University Press, 1999).

Martin Durham teaches politics at the University of Wolverhampton. He is the author of *Women and Fascism* (Routledge, London, 1998) and *The Christian Right, the Far Right and the Boundaries of American Conservatism* (Manchester University Press, Manchester, 2000).

Michael Murphy has edited a collection of George Garrett's writings (*The Collected George Garrett*, Trent Editions, Nottingham, 1999). He has just completed his doctoral thesis on the connections between exile and poetry post–1939.

Matt Perry teaches history at the University of Sunderland. He is the author of *Bread and Work: The experience of unemployment 1918–39* (Pluto, London, 2000) and *Marxism and History* (Palgrave, forthcoming).

David Renton teaches history at Edge Hill College of Higher Education. He is the author of *Marx on Globalisation* (Lawrence and Wishart, London, 2001) and *This Rough Game: Fascism and anti-Fascism* (Sutton, 2001).

Duncan Thompson recently completed a PhD at Brighton University on the history of the *New Left Review*.

Editorial

In his work on collective memory, cited by Michael Murphy in the present issue, Maurice Halbwachs wrote that the past 'is not preserved but is reconstructed on the basis of the present'. Of course, traces of the past are preserved, and it is on these traces that historians base their claims to insight and authenticity. On the other hand, it is unquestionably true that they do so 'on the basis of the present', and that their reconstructions are continuously in process of revision over time and subject to controversies which inform and derive from conflicting responses to contemporary agendas. The legacies of the past are always subject to contested claims, and it is by advancing these competing claims that we help determine what these legacies are.

In Perry Anderson's recent mission statement for the 'new' *New Left Review*, Duncan Thompson claims that Anderson did not offer a critical reevaluation of *NLR*'s own intellectual legacy, and what this legacy might mean for those hoping for something more than a worldly-wise mood of resignation. Thompson argues, it is Anderson's famed Olympianism which might have helped place in a longer perspective the present ascendancy of neo-liberalism.

Mark Bevir's contribution offers a longer perspective on the intellectual legacies of the British left which has an obvious contemporary resonance. Focusing on the fraught relationship between socialism and traditional liberalism, he shows that socialists turned to both the state and associationism to compensate for the inequities of the market. In recent years, preoccupations with the first of these have assisted in the discrediting of socialism, at least in the guise of the command economies of the Soviet bloc. Bevir's account reminds us that there are alternative traditions, rooted he says in writers like Cole and Laski, which continue to provide resources for socialist alternatives.

The articles of Matt Perry and Michael Murphy both focus on the British hunger marches of the 1930s. Matt Perry considers two great unemployed demonstrations of 1936, one the famous 'Jarrow Crusade' indelibly associated with the town's MP, Ellen Wilkinson, and the other the National Hunger March organised by the communist-led National Unemployed Workers' Movement. Drawing on new evidence, Perry contests prevailing judgements that the Jarrow march was the more effective of the two, and ascribes these judgements to a historical orthodoxy unwilling to accept that 'extremism' may not always have been such a failure in inter-war Britain—and to judge from Perry's account, may not always have been so extreme either.

Michael Murphy takes issue with a similar sort of convention in relation to 1930's literature. The established canon of the 'red decade', he points out, is dominated by middle-class literary figures like 'Macspaunday', the facetious Oxford amalgam of W.H. Auden, Stephen Spender, C. Day-Lewis and Louis MacNeice. Murphy on the other hand is concerned with a different sort of writer: the unemployed seaman and former Wobbly, George Garrett, whom George Orwell encountered in Liverpool while researching *The Road to Wigan Pier* in 1936. Having recently edited a critical edition of Garrett's writings, Murphy here continues the process of recovery by exploring the use of memory and experience in Garrett's writings of the 1930s—including a retrospective account of a 1920's hunger march, which may in part have been stimulated by the more recent episodes described in Matt Perry's article.

Finally, fascism is a legacy we need to confront, not just on the basis of the present but of our possible futures. How to neutralise the possible appeals of the extreme right has long given rise to controversy on the left, and the issue's political sensitivity continues to give an edge to scholarly debates which can never be entirely academic. In this issue we give an airing to one of these, focusing on the relationship between women, gender and fascism. While all historians acknowledge that fascism appealed to very considerable numbers of women, David Renton in his critique of certain trends in the recent literature rejects any suggestion that this significantly qualifies or extenuates the movement's basic hostility to women's rights. Martin Durham, in response, draws on his own extensive research to argue that the relations between fascism and gender varied according to time and place and were contested from within fascism itself. They cannot, he argues, invariably be characterised as anti-feminist. Neither contributor refers to contemporary events, but the exchange inevitably acquires a greater immediacy due to recent developments in Austria, Italy and, closer to home, in Oldham. While assessments of these developments will vary, thinking in terms of epochs and continents does at least provide a salutary antidote to complacency as well as despair.

Of the reviews which follow, several take up the theme of contested legacies: of fascism, the Cold War, women's suffrage and of the personal legacies of major intellectual figures such as Edward Thompson. Readers interested in contributing reviews are encouraged to send a note of their interests to Stephen Woodhams at the e-mail address provided. While we cannot accept unsolicited reviews, we are always looking to add names to our pool of reviewers.

Socialism, Civil Society and the State in Modern Britain[1]

Mark Bevir

Any adequate discussion of the changing nature of western European states during the twentieth century should include accounts of both the expansion of their role and the democratisation of their structure. On one hand, they became increasingly centralised and took on new functions in ways that strengthened them in relation to civil society. The British state concentrated decision making in itself, added to its jurisdictions, increased taxation, extended its powers of surveillance, developed new strategies of economic management, oversaw massive growth in the public sector, and accepted some responsibility for the welfare of its citizens. On the other hand, however, many western European states, especially after 1945, granted new political and social rights to their citizens in ways that made them increasingly subject to popular, democratic control. The British state was transformed by the growing power of representative institutions, the establishment of universal adult suffrage, the introduction of legal protections for trade unions, and the embodiment of social rights within the welfare state.

These changes in western European states have been explored mainly in relation to theories of economic development: Marxists have emphasised the rise of monopoly capitalism, non-Marxists the rise of corporate capitalism. Similarly, the coterminous changes in civil society, including the economy, have been explored mainly in relation to theories of the state: scholars have emphasised the impact on social life of the way states mobilised their citizens for war, the extension of disciplinary power from state institutions to social practices, and the growth of rational bureaucracies.[2] Another way of approaching these changes, however, is in the context of changes in ideas or culture. This approach will have the great advantage of enabling us to explain the apparent paradox of an expansion of state power being accompanied by a wave of democratisation. This essay, then, will make two main arguments. The first is that socialist theories criticised the free market and thereby undermined the intellectual foundations of the liberal ideal of civil society.

Socialists argued that the market was not a naturally harmonious system, so either the state or associations in civil society had to work to correct its defects. The second thesis is that as socialists rejected the free market, they looked to associations in civil society and popular democratic control of the state to protect the interests of the individual. The spread of socialist ideas therefore led both to new powers being taken on by the state and to an extension of the rights of the citizen against the state.

To relate the changing nature of the state and civil society to socialist ideas is to complicate our understanding of the relationship of political, social, and intellectual forces. Civil society incorporates beliefs, meanings, and debates that inform the public activities of individuals, groups, and institutions in ways that transform the political sphere. Equally, however, because these beliefs, meanings, and debates arise from reflections on social and political forces, the state and associations in civil society act in ways that transform the intellectual inquiries found in civil society. The suggestion here is that we can not analyze the dialectical relationship between civil society and the state in terms of objective social and political categories. Rather, we have to see civil society and the state as moderating one another within the context of evolving intellectual traditions. Different forms of civil society and the state develop together as the historical products of beliefs and debates. Here the Enlightenment promoted a faith in a market economy as a harmonious and self-regulating system. A liberal commitment to the minimal state, laissez-faire, and free trade inspired many people to try, with some success, to withdraw the state from the economic sphere of civic life. But the attempt to realise the liberal ideal, including an experience of a market economy, led socialists and others to reconceptualise the state and civil society. These new analyses of the state and civil society then set the scene for the rise of social-democratic states.

In what follows, civil society will be understood broadly to include all groups and institutions that lie between, on one hand, household and kinship groups and, on the other, the state.[3] Because civil society exists alongside the family and the state, it overlaps with them in ways that prevent us from making any rigid distinctions here. Still, the general contours of a broad concept of civil society are clear. Under this broad concept, moreover, economic institutions, including a market economy, are part of civil society, though not constitutive of it. A broad concept of civil society embraces liberal instances in which a market economy plays an important role, other instances in which there is little market activity, and a range of possibilities between these two extremes. Indeed, the shift from classical liberalism to socialism centered on the extent to which the market could contribute to the good of society. Liberals and socialists alike typically believed in the benefits of a strong associational culture, though within both camps there were disagreements about the merits of particular associations, such as churches and trade unions. But whereas classical liberals usually advocated a large role for the market economy as part of civil society, socialists did not. Debates about the workings of the market economy were, therefore, central to the shift from classical liberalism to social democracy.

Benefits of the market economy

The establishment of a civil society placed outside of the legitimate demands of the state was a specific historical achievement. The cultural roots of this achievement lay in moral and pragmatic claims for religious liberties and in the claims of merchants and artisans to similar liberties. Claims to personal freedom were extended from intimate matters to religion and also to economic activities. Moreover, these latter claims arose as states undertook increasingly onerous military functions in part to open up and then protect foreign trade. A Puritan emphasis on personal conduct fed into a new capitalist discourse focused on the productive citizen so as to generate a vigorous defence of a liberal civil society.[4] In the eighteenth century, various social theorists reworked this defence to incorporate the Newtonian idea of the universe as a system of forces. Civil society, and more especially economic activity, was seen as a harmonious and self-regulating system akin to the planets. Theorists of the Scottish Enlightenment, such as Adam Smith, and later on utilitarians, including J.S. Mill, argued that private activity, whether based on habit or self-interest, could optimise wealth and happiness as well as secure peace and prosperity. Classical liberalism asserted that the economic sphere within civil society could be left to itself. A market economy would bring not an anarchic muddle but a near perfect social system.

It is possible, of course, to overstate the extent to which classical liberals put their faith in an unregulated civil society. For a start, many classical liberals were as profoundly concerned with civic virtue as with individual freedom, and they looked to associations within civil society to sustain and to embody such virtue.[5] Mill saw civic activities, especially participation in local government, as vital to ensure social solidarity. Indeed, he sympathised with Samuel Coleridge's notion of a clerisy and Auguste Comte's notion of a religion of humanity to such an extent that we can describe him as an aristocratic liberal anxious to ameliorate the possible effects of democracy.[6] He argued that representative government required a particular type of political culture, which, therefore, should be promoted as a civic religion. 'Hardly any language,' he wrote, 'is strong enough to express the strength of my conviction—on the importance of that portion of the operation of free institutions, which may be called the public education of the citizens.'[7] In addition, many classical liberals expressed serious concerns about the impact of the market upon civic culture. The thinkers of the Scottish Enlightenment, notably Sir James Steuart and Adam Ferguson, were worried about the public effects of the place that luxury acquired within modern economies.[8] Later Mill actually argued 'that the most serious danger to the future prospects of mankind is in the unbalanced influence of the commercial spirit.'[9] He believed that only thorough participation in the detailed business of government could prevent the commercial spirit from creating a mean populace bereft of civic virtue. Despite such forebodings, however, classical liberals generally extolled the benefits of the market economy. The thinkers of the Scottish Enlightenment, most famously Adam Smith, were modernisers who sought to show how the operation of the market transformed self-interested actions into public goods. Likewise, Mill defended a basic adherence to the market rather than state intervention on grounds that were common among the philosophical radicals. He wrote: 'the great majority of things are worse done by the intervention of government, than the individuals interested in the matter would do them, or cause them to be done, if left to themselves.'[10] When all the necessary caveats have been made, therefore, we are left with the fact that classical liberals placed their faith in the market. They defended the market in debates with their contemporaries, and they believed, more than any group of thinkers before them, that an unregulated economy could provide prosperity, peace, and happiness. Classical liberalism is rightly associated with advocacy of a large role for a market economy. No doubt we can debate the extent to which the nineteenth-century state actually did withdraw from the economy, let alone other areas of civil society, but the fact remains that the dominant discourse and broad thrust of public policy pointed in such a direction. Victorian Britain came to stand for the classical-liberal vision of a minimal state, laissez-faire, and free trade. However, even as classical liberalism became a dominant belief system in British society, so people began to conceive of dilemmas within its account of the world. Not everybody recognised the salience of the dilemmas, let alone understood them to require a rejection of liberal doctrine. But socialists did so, and even liberals often recognised their import and sought to modify their beliefs accordingly. Three main dilemmas stand out. The first was a moral concern with the way the market economy undermined the traditional values and associations that made for a stable society. Romantics and radical Tories often argued that liberalism actually promoted disharmony and discord. They called for a more orderly and just civil society, with the state both sponsoring associations, such as Coleridge's clerisy, designed to promulgate civic virtue, and also intervening to protect vulnerable industries and communities.[11]

The second dilemma arose in classical economics. In the 1850s and 1860s, trade unions expanded, wages and living standards rose, and there was a population boom. Such conjunctions made a mockery of the classical theory of distribution. If trade unions could raise wages, one had to reject the wages-fund theory according to which in the short term there was a fixed amount of savings to pay wages. And if population and living standards could rise simultaneously, one had to reject the law of 'natural' subsistence wages, according to which population growth responded to wage rates so as to bring them back to subsistence level. Economists experienced a crisis within their discipline—even J.S. Mill rejected the wages-fund theory.[12] The final dilemma appeared in the widespread belief that trade cycles produced inevitable slumps. Many observers believed that Britain experienced just such a slump from the early 1870s to the early 1890s.[13] They often complained that the British economy suffered from a range of ills, including technological obsolescence, insufficient investment, myopic entrepreneurs, poor management, and, most significantly, a lack of support from the state. Although reflecting on these dilemmas did not require one to reject classical liberalism, let alone to adopt socialism, the socialist critique of classical liberalism did arise in large part out of reflections on these dilemmas. Indeed, we might almost say that British Marxism embodied a concern with economic cycles, Fabianism a concern to rework classical economics, and ethical socialism a moral critique of the disruptive effects of the market.

Failings of the market economy

In the mid- and late-Victorian age, radicals more or less accepted the classical-liberal vision of a harmonious and self-regulating market economy. Their critique of British society drew on a republican tradition in which social ills appeared as products of a corrupt political system rather than the inner workings of the economy.[14] Radicals argued that the undemocratic, oligarchic nature of the British state enabled landlords and moneylords to institutionalise an unnatural and unjust distribution of land and thereby to keep a virtuous people in poverty. During the 1880s, however, popular radicals began to turn to Marxism in a way that led them to break with this republican tradition. Certainly the Marxists of the Social Democratic Federation (SDF), the Socialist League, and the Bloomsbury Socialist Society began to describe social ills as products of an exploitation integral to capitalism.[15] Early British Marxists adopted Marx's catastrophist vision of capitalist development. They argued that the market economy was leading not to happiness, wealth, and peace but to crises of overproduction, the immiserisation of workers, and imperial rivalries.[16] Capitalist competition led to the accumulation and concentration of capital, which then increased productive capacity. But because this increased production soon outstripped demand, capitalists were then forced into ever harsher competition, which soon led to a crisis characterised by bankruptcies, cutbacks, and unemployment. Here the growth of fixed capital, the pressure to reduce costs, and unemployment all forced wages down, thereby leading to the immiserisation of the workers and the further accumulation of capital. Similarly, the intensity of competition prompted capitalists both to use the state to secure markets through imperialism and to seek refuge in trusts and cartels that further concentrated capital. Before long, however, the further accumulation and concentration of capital led to an even worse economic crisis. The free market was self-destructive, not self-regulating.

British Marxists rejected the idea of the market economy as a harmonious and self-regulating sphere. Indeed, many of them believed that the failings of capitalism made state intervention in civil society essential. H.M. Hyndman evoked a 'principle of State management' in 1881 just after reading Marx.[17] Soon afterwards, at the founding meeting of the SDF, he issued a pamphlet with the significant title *The Text Book of Democracy*. The pamphlet argued that 'the time is coming when all will be able to recognise that its [the state's] friendly influence is needed to prevent serious trouble, and lead the way to a happier period.'[18] When British Marxists rejected the idea that the market economy guarantees individual liberty and social cohesion, they argued not only that the state had to intervene in civil society to secure a just and stable society but also that freedom had to be secured by a democratic political system. Hyndman insisted that 'a great democratic English Republic has ever been the dream of the noblest of our race,' and 'to bring about such a Republic is the cause for which we Socialists agitate to-day.'[19] The program of the SDF called not only for a parliament based on universal suffrage but for popular control of this parliament to be reinforced through measures such as annual elections, referenda, a principle of delegation, abolition of the House of Lords, and even an elected civil service.

Although Marxists often accepted the need for a more interventionist state, their economic theory did not compel them to do so. Because the evils of capitalism arose from private ownership of the means of production, a civil society without such ownership might conceivably come to resemble the liberal ideal of a harmonious and self-regulating system. The crucial question for Marxists, therefore, was what form common ownership of the means of production should take. While members of the SDF generally believed that a democratic state could act as a suitable vehicle for common ownership, other Marxists were more hostile to the state. Socialist, poet, and designer William Morris, for example, defended a form of anarcho-communism. The absence of private property would remove almost all cause for disagreement so that civil society could become a self-regulating sphere from which politics would be more or less absent.[20] Other Marxists, notably Tom Mann, favored a form of syndicalism: they gave an extended role to the state, while unpacking its democratic structure in terms of industrial units composed of producers, not geographical units composed of citizens.[21]

The SDF appealed almost exclusively to popular and Tory radicals. Liberal radical converts to socialism, in contrast, often joined the Fabian Society. They did so in the context of the collapse of classical economics.[22] During the 1870s and 1880s, economists such as W. S. Jevons and Alfred Marshall developed various versions of marginalist economics. Fabians such as George Bernard Shaw and Sidney Webb then drew on marginalism to construct theories of rent as exploitation.[23] Shaw argued that capitalists exploited workers in part by the exercise of their monopoly of the means of production and in part because as landlords they appropriated the rents arising from natural advantages of fertility. Webb argued that interest was strictly analogous to land rent since it derived from an advantageous industrial situation. Both Shaw and Webb believed, therefore, that any economy necessarily produced rent understood as a social surplus. Rent was unearned in that it reflected natural or social variations of fertility or industrial situation. Moreover, rent did not contribute to the maintenance of the supply of land or capital necessary to the efficient functioning of the economy but, rather, appeared when there was a permanent or temporary quasi monopoly. As Webb explained, 'an additional product determined by the relative differences in the productive efficiency of the different sites, soils, capitals and forms of skill above the margin has gone to those exercising control over those valuable but scarce productive forces.'[24] Indeed, the Fabians believed that rent promoted economic inefficiencies. According to Sidney and Beatrice Webb, child labour, variable local rates, and so forth generated forms of rent or 'bounties' that enabled inefficient companies to flourish.[25] The free market led to an uncoordinated industrial system composed of numerous fragmented centres of management that knew little about each other's activities. The anarchic nature of capitalism resulted in duplication, temporary blockages, and other unnecessary forms of waste. Capitalism, the Fabians concluded, was unjust and inefficient, not harmonious and self-regulating.

Fabian economic theories, unlike those of the Marxists, virtually compelled their adherents to call for a more interventionist state. Crucially, rent arose not just under capitalism but within any economy. The surplus value evoked by Marx arose from the buying and selling of labour in a capitalist economy, so collective ownership of the means of production would eliminate it irrespective of the particular role given to the state. The rents evoked by the Fabians, in contrast, arose from the variable productivity of different lands and, arguably, capitals. The solution, therefore, was for the state to appropriate rent.[26] As Shaw explained, 'economic rent, arising as it does from variations of fertility or advantages of situation, must always be held as common or social wealth, and used, as the revenues raised by taxation are now used, for public purposes.'[27] The Fabians did not believe that the extended role they advocated for the state need bring an increase in bureaucracy. On the contrary, they suggested that state action would eliminate the wasteful inefficiencies of a market economy. The Fabians acknowledged, however, that socialism would make the integrity and efficiency of the state absolutely vital, and they saw democracy as the best means to secure an honest state. They hoped 'through Democracy to gather the whole people into the State, so that the State may be trusted with the rent of the country.'[28] Yet because the Fabians generally drew on the liberalism of Bentham and Mill, not the republicanism that fed into the SDF, they defined democracy as representative government almost to the exclusion of other forms of popular control over the executive.

The third strand to make up British socialism was an ethical one based principally on a moral critique of capitalism. Ethical socialists, following Thomas Carlyle and John Ruskin, denounced the free market and competition in favour of a moral economy and cooperation.[29] Proponents of the moral economy rejected the classical-liberal view of the market economy as a road to prosperity, happiness, and peace. They associated it instead with poverty, urban squalor, immorality, and social dislocation. Even if it did bring material benefits, these were outweighed by its social costs. Besides, many of the commodities produced in a market economy met artificial wants, not genuine needs, since production in it responded primarily to the changing whims and fashions of the wealthy. Perhaps the worst facet of the market, however, was its promotion of individualism and competition; it brought to the fore people's mean and selfish instincts as opposed to their generous and sharing ones. Edward Carpenter complained of self-consciousness being 'almost a disease; when the desire of acquiring and grasping objects, or of enslaving men and animals, in order to administer to the self, becomes one of the main motives of life.'[30] Capitalism elevated material greed above human relationships.

Ethical socialists rarely evoked sophisticated economic theories to reveal the unjust or inefficient nature of capitalism. Indeed, Carpenter dismissed the debate over the nature of value as akin to disputes among medieval scholastics.[31] The important thing was not to provide some formal theory of abstract economic processes but to examine the actual results of these processes and then to assess their moral acceptability. Ethical socialists wanted everyone to acknowledge that, in Wilfrid Richmond's words, 'economies are within the sphere of conscience.'[32] For many of them, the appropriate sphere of conscience derived from an immanentist Christianity, as with Richmond, or a mystical belief in the unity of all things, as with Carpenter. God was present in all of us, uniting us in a single brotherhood, the ethical expression of which was a social fellowship that required us to concern ourselves with others in all our daily activities. The welfare of others constituted the central focus of the moral economy.[33] Capitalists, consumers, and workers alike had to put the well-being of their fellows before selfish concerns with profits, prices, and wages. The liberal view of civil society, with the powerful role it ascribed to the market, stood condemned, therefore, for its failure to ground economics on an ethic of co-operative fellowship.

The idea of a moral economy had perilously little to say about the role of the state under socialism. Ethical socialists typically defined socialism as the enactment of a spirit of democracy, fellowship, or brotherhood. Carpenter spoke of realising the 'instinct of loving Union which lies at the root of every human Soul.'[34] The Christian Social Union, more concretely, promoted 'white lists' of producers and retailers who met specified criteria with respect to fair wages, decent working conditions, and so forth.[35] By dealing exclusively with such producers and retailers, socialists put the welfare of others before their own wealth and thus laid the foundations for the moral economy. The ethical socialists' ideal centered on a personal democracy in which relationships were based on equality and love. The particular role of the state was of little importance compared to personal transformations and the consequent revolution in civil society. On one hand, if economic interactions were governed by suitable moral values, there would be little need for the state to intervene. Thus, Carpenter advocated a non-governmental society based on cooperative units of production.[36] On the other hand, however, debates about the economic role to be played by the state should not be allowed to detract from the vital need for a moral revolution within civil society. Thus, Carpenter argued that all forms of socialism and anarchism embodied the same ideal, and the key thing was to spread the ideal without worrying about the material form it might take.[37] Similarly, Christian socialists evoked the example of Christ: 'Our Lord...preached no system of political economy. He never for a moment would allow us to suppose that changes in the machinery of political life or in the distribution of wealth would remedy the fundamental evils of society. What he required was a profound ethical change based on thoughts about God and about man.'[38]

The role of the state

Socialists reconceptualised the market economy in ways that led them to reject the classical liberal vision of civil society. Some socialists, notably the Fabians and many Marxists, argued that the state had to take on new functions and play a more active role in civil society. They called for an extension of democracy to ensure that a more active state remained trustworthy. Other socialists, notably the ethical socialists and some Marxists, argued that civil society needed to be purged of abuses associated with competitive individualism and capitalism. They called for the democratization of civil society itself: for the ethical socialists, civil society needed to embody the democratic spirit of true fellowship; for Marxists attracted to syndicalism, the associations in civil society needed to be made thoroughly democratic.[39] One of the main debates among British socialists, therefore, concerned the relative roles to be played under socialism by a democratic state and democratic associations in civil society. To simplify, we might say that the dominant outlook in the Independent Labour Party and the Labour Party fused ethical socialism with Fabian economics to emphasise the role of the state, but that this dominant outlook was criticised by socialists influenced by syndicalist forms of Marxism and non-governmental forms of ethical socialism.

Leading figures in the Labour Party—Keir Hardie, Philip Snowden, and Ramsay MacDonald—condemned capitalism in much the same terms as the ethical socialists. Snowden condemned the competitive market for bringing out our 'animal instincts,' not our moral ones: 'it makes men hard, cruel, selfish, acquisitive economic machines.'[40] MacDonald defended the idea of 'buying in the best market,' where the idea of 'the best' had to include the welfare of producers, not just cheapness.[41] And Hardie evoked the Sermon on the Mount and spoke of the coming of the Kingdom of God. Within the framework of ethical socialism, however, leading figures in the Labour Party turned to the Fabians to provide them with an economic analysis of the market economy. Snowden followed Webb's theory of interest as analogous to land rent, arguing that 'just as the landlord gets an unearned income from the increase in the value of land, so the capitalist gets an unearned increment from improvements in productive methods and in other ways not the result of his own efforts or abilities.'[42] And MacDonald followed the Webbs's denunciation of the uncoordinated nature of the market, arguing that, whereas capitalism relied on a haphazard and chaotic clash of individual interests, socialism would eliminate waste by organising economic life on a scientific basis.[43]

The Labour Party's reliance on Fabian economics led it to reject the ideal of an unregulated civil society and instead to demand various forms of state intervention. For a start, the existence of an unearned increment present in all economies suggested that the state should be in charge of collecting this surplus and using it for the benefit of the community. The Labour Party's mock budget of 1907, for example, spoke of introducing 'taxation' so as to collect 'unearned…increments of wealth' and use them 'for communal benefit.'[44] Hardie, MacDonald, and Snowden advocated a range of measures to deal with the social surplus in the economy. To secure the surplus, they wanted not only taxation but also legislative restrictions on property rights and eventually public ownership of the means of production. To deploy the surplus for communal benefit, they wanted a considerable extension of social welfare legislation. In addition, they advocated public ownership of the means of production in order to end the anarchic nature of capitalist production. The solution to both overproduction and unemployment lay in the state taking control of the economy and regulating supply in relation to demand.

The leading figures in the Labour Party turned to the state to correct the failings they believed were inherent in the market economy. They rejected traditional fears about a too-powerful state by stressing the ethical nature of a truly democratic state. Liberals had been right to oppose state intervention when the state had been a corrupt aristocratic one, but the establishment of democracy would make the state trustworthy. As MacDonald explained, 'the democratic State is an organisation of the people, democratic government is self-government, democratic law is an expression of the will of the people who have to obey the law.'[45] The leading figures within the Labour Party defined democracy in terms taken again from the ethical socialists and the Fabians. They equated democracy with a spirit of fellowship and representative institutions, rarely showing enthusiasm for other forms of popular control of the state. A social-democratic state provided a vehicle for freedom. The liberal view of liberty as based on individual activity in a civil society undisturbed by the state made sense when such activity was believed to yield justice, wealth, peace, and happiness. But once socialists questioned the efficacy of the market as a deliverer of such goods, they had to redefine the value of liberty. Typically they redefined it as dependent on factors such as employment, a minimal standard of welfare, and even participation in a polity aiming at the common good. The state became a vehicle for promoting liberty.

While the dominant outlook in the Labour Party drew on Fabian economics, socialist opposition to this outlook often drew on forms of Marxism drifting towards syndicalism and forms of ethical socialism incorporating a non-governmental ideal. The leading British syndicalists, including Mann and James Connolly, were Marxists who had belonged to the SDF.[46] They emphasised two themes. They argued, first, that the cure for capitalism lay in a transformation of industry and society without any involvement by the political realm. Because Marxist economics did not compel one to call for a greater role for the state, syndicalists were able to envisage a harmonious civil society in which the capitalist system of private property had been replaced by one based on worker-owned industrial units. The syndicalists rejected the Labour Party's commitment to realising socialism through a parliamentary party and, instead, looked toward the industrial action of trade unions. The syndicalists argued, second, that any leadership soon became a self-serving bureaucracy unless it were subject to strong democratic control. Even worker-owned industrial units had to be subject to popular control through a principle of delegation and so forth. The syndicalists, and many other Marxists, opposed the Labour Party's restricted view of democracy as requiring little other than representative government.[47] They wanted to extend popular control by introducing the initiative and referenda into the institutions with which they were concerned.

Ethical socialism, with its debt to Ruskin, often incorporated a romantic medievalism in which craftsmen conjoined in guilds were seen as an approximation to the ideal of a social fellowship. A.J. Penty developed this medievalism in his *The Restoration of the Gild System*, which in its preface acknowledged a debt to Ruskin and to Carpenter and which inspired the other begetters of guild socialism, A.R. Orage and S.G. Hobson.[48] The early guild socialists drew on two themes central to the ethical socialist tradition. They argued, first, that the ideal of fellowship consisted of a social spirit of democracy. Individuals would exercise full control over their own daily activities in a cooperative and decentralised society. As Penty explained, 'it is necessary to transfer the control of industry from the hands of the financier into those of the craftsman.'[49] The guild socialists argued, second, that the cure for capitalism lay in this moral ideal of fellowship, an ideal to which the political realm was largely irrelevant and perhaps even detrimental. Because the moral economy did not require state intervention, indeed because state-owned industries were capable of retaining the commercial ethic of private companies, the Labour Party should focus not on parliamentary politics but on the creation of the ideal of fellowship. The guild socialists rejected the Labour Party's view of democracy as representative government. Democracy, they insisted, entailed local control over the institutions within civil society and these institutions being largely autonomous from the state.

The Labour Party called for an extension of the state to eliminate the inequities and inefficiencies associated with capitalism. Socialist hostility to this position, from both within and outside the party, drew on the economics of the Marxists and ethical socialists to defend socialist visions based on voluntary associations rather than the state.[50] Although all socialists rejected the classical-liberal ideal, there was a division between those who looked to the state to correct the failings of the market and those who sought to transform civil society from within itself in a way that would make state intervention superfluous. The latter group long continued to criticise the Labour Party for the statist nature of its ideal and its limited concept of democracy. Not long after the end of the First World War, for instance, pluralists such as G.D.H. Cole and Harold Laski fused guild socialism with syndicalism, and also some Fabian themes, in an attempt to revitalise the democratic impulses within the Labour Party.[51]

Social-democracy and its discontents

By the outbreak of the First World War, the Labour Party had accepted socialist doctrines that committed it to an extended role for the state. These doctrines transformed state and society over the next half-century. To understand why these doctrines did so, however, we have to recognise that closely related ones gained ground among non-socialists.[52] Both liberals and conservatives reflected on the dilemmas posed by economic cycles, marginalism, and a moral disquiet at the effects of the market. When they did so, they often adopted ideas resembling those of the socialists. Thus, J.A. Hobson explained cycles in the economy as products of a form of underconsumption endemic to the free market, while Marshall introduced the concepts of producer's and consumer's surpluses into neoclassical economics.[53] Numerous theorists began to challenge the idea that the market constituted a harmonious, self-regulating system. Moreover, they often turned to the state to put right the failings of the market, and to democracy to ensure the state could be trusted to play such a role. It is not surprising, therefore, that the twentieth century has witnessed both an expansion of state power and a growth of democracy. The state increased taxation, took an increasingly active role in economic management, and accepted some responsibility for the welfare of its citizens precisely because the market economy was now conceived as incapable of dealing adequately with such matters. Equally, the suffrage was extended, legal protections were granted to institutions in civil society such as trade unions, and citizens acquired greater social rights against the state precisely because an extended state was conceived as being trustworthy only if it were subject to democratic control.

The changes in the nature of the state and civil society therefore have to be located against the relevant intellectual background. No doubt the rise of corporate capitalism, the need of the state to mobilise the population for war, and similar factors played a role in bringing about the changes. Nonetheless, these developments were not given to people as brute facts; rather, they were developments that people made sense of through beliefs and debates that constituted part of the intellectual background. Certainly one need not conceive of trusts and cartels as in need of regulation, let alone as evidence of the need for state ownership. Socialists and others argued in this way only because public debate, private discussion, and personal reflection led them to reject the liberal view of civil society that dominated Victorian Britain. Similarly, politicians would not have mobilised people for war through the state if they had believed the state could not play such a role, and they would not have seen the experience of war as relevant for peace had they not been convinced there were problems with a market economy. The First World War mattered because it was interpreted as further evidence of the failings of a classical liberalism that already had been rejected. MacDonald said that the war provided 'a wonderful proof' of the socialist argument, not that the war constituted the socialist argument.[54] The war reinforced arguments about the inequity and inefficiency of the free market, arguments that pointed the way to a shift in vision from a market economy and night-watchman state to social democracy.

Of course, the process of historical change has continued throughout the twentieth century. The emergence of new ideas and institutions produced new debates. Social theorists theorised dilemmas in the theory and practice of social democracy, and these theories inspired further changes in both state and civil society. Social theorists began to suggest that social democracy had undermined civil society. Many of them went on to equate the alleged decline of civil society with an apparent lack of social cohesion. Moreover, worries about the erosion of social cohesion were compounded by a growing unease over the operation of the welfare state. Social theorists began to highlight the emergence of an underclass trapped in a cycle of welfare dependency. Some theorists also argued that the bureaucratic nature of the welfare state undermined the spirit of independence and self-help among many of its beneficiaries. The solution to all of these problems has often been seen to lie in a vigourous civil society. In this view, the welfare state needs to be superseded, at least to some extent, by voluntary associations based on local initiatives. Some of the theorists who call for a revitalised civil society are part of the new right; people like David Green generally adopt a neo-liberal vision that relies heavily on the market.[55] Others, however, are inspired by the arguments with which syndicalists and guild socialists once challenged the dominant ideas in the Labour Party. Paul Hirst, for example, has drawn on Cole, J. N. Figgis, and Laski to argue for a shift from the state to a more pluralist society. He wants to revitalise civil society by returning to it tasks currently undertaken by the state and by thoroughly democratising its institutions and practices.[56] In Britain, however, most critics of the existing social-democratic state still allow, albeit tacitly, some validity to the arguments of the early Fabians and ethical socialists. Certainly neither Green nor Hirst wants to do away with the welfare state altogether. Rather, they want to see the state doing more through and alongside markets or democratic associations. Therefore the arguments of the early socialists still constitute a part of the accepted background against which current disputes are conducted.

Notes

1. An earlier version of this essay appeared in F. Trentmann (ed.), *Paradoxes of Civil Society* (New York, 2000), pp.332–51.
2. See, respectively, Theda Skocpol, *Protecting Soldiers and Mothers. The political origins of social policy in the United States* (Cambridge, MA, 1992); Michel Foucault, *Discipline and Punish. The birth of the prison*, transl. A. Sheridan Smith (London, 1977); Max Weber, *On Capitalism, Bureaucracy, and Religion*, ed. S. Andreski (London, 1983).
3. Some scholars define civil society in contrast to the market. See, e.g., Jean Cohen and Andrew Arato, *Civil Society and Political Theory* (Cambridge, MA, 1992). While we should not confuse issues of definition with those of substance, I am worried that this way of defining the term encourages certain assumptions about clear-cut differences between the market and other aspects of civil society. Consider, for instance, three plausible reasons for defining civil society in contrast to the market. First, one might say the market lacks the personal immediacy, or face-to-face interactions, of some associations. Surely, however, the market entails such interactions when consumers buy items in shops or workers negotiate with managers; and surely a number of churches are constituted more by television and radio programs than by physical meetings. The level of personal intimacy in an institution depends on the technology associated with it as much as on any properties allegedly intrinsic to it. Second, one might say people do not join the market in the way they do other associations. But surely people are brought into both churches and markets by learning and repeating appropriate patterns of behavior in a process of socialization. Likewise, to suggest that people choose to join other associations in a way they do not the market is to come perilously close to assuming a view of the human subject as autonomous, when such a view is at best ethnocentric and at worst unsustainable. Third, one might suggest that other associations perform functions different than the market performs in society. Surely, however, all sorts of associations are capable of performing all sorts of functions. To equate certain associations with certain functions is, therefore, again to run the risk of creating a theory that is at best ethnocentric and at worst unsustainable. Cf. Chris Hann

and Elizabeth Dunn (eds), *Civil Society. Challenging Western Models* (London, 1996). No doubt there are differences, at least of degree, here. But by insisting on including the market within civil society, we help to dispel some of the mythic qualities ascribed to the market by both its proponents and its critics.
4. The classic study of the process remains Max Weber, *The Protestant Ethic and the Spirit of Capitalism*, trans. T. Parsons, intro. R. Tawney (London, 1930).
5. Donald Winch, *Adam Smith's Politics* (Cambridge, 1978); Eugenio Biagini, 'Liberalism and direct democracy: John Stuart Mill and the model of ancient Athens', in E. Biagini (ed.), *Citizenship and Community: Liberals, Radicals, and collective identities in the British Isles, 1865–1931* (Cambridge, 1996), pp.21–44. It should be said, however, that by the time we reach Mill the idea of virtue has been transformed to highlight self-development and responsible public participation.
6. Alan Kahan, *Aristocratic Liberalism. The social and political thought of Jacob Burckhardt, John Stuart Mill, and Alexis de Tocqueville* (Oxford, 1992).
7. J.S. Mill, 'Considerations on representative government', in *Collected Works of J. S. Mill* (London, 1963/89), vol.19, p.535.
8. Istvan Hont, 'The rich country-poor country debate in Scottish classical political economy', in I. Hont and M. Ignatieff (eds), *Wealth and Virtue. The shaping of political economy in the Scottish Enlightenment* (Cambridge, 1983).
9. J. S. Mill, 'De Tocqueville on democracy in America [II]', in *Collected Works*, vol.18, p.198.
10. J. S. Mill, 'Principles of political economy', in *Collected Works*, vol.3, p.941.
11. Jonathan Mendilow, *The Romantic Tradition in British Politics* (London, 1986); Raymond Williams, *Culture and Society, 1780–1950* (London, 1987).
12. J. S. Mill, 'Thornton on Labour and its claims', in *Collected Works*, vol. 5, pp.631–68. Examples of economists decrying the state of their discipline include William Cunningham, 'Political economy as a moral science', *Mind*, 3, 1878, pp.369–83; H. S. Foxwell, 'The economic movement in England', *Quarterly Journal of Economics*, 2, 1888, pp.84–103; Henry Sidgwick, *The Principles of Political Economy* (London, 1883), pp.1–7.
13. Historians have been skeptical about the depth of the depression, restricting it at most to certain sectors: see S. B. Saul, *The Myth of the Great Depression 1873–1896* (London, 1969). The fact remains, however, that most contemporaries believed they were living through a depression.
14. The alliance between radicals and liberals has been emphasised by Eugenio Biagini and Alastair Reid (eds), *Currents of Radicalism. Popular radicalism, organised labour and party politics in Britain, 1850–1914* (Cambridge, 1991). On the discourse of popular radicalism, see Patrick Joyce, *Visions of the People. Industrial England and the question of class* (Cambridge, 1991); Gareth Stedman Jones, 'Rethinking Chartism', in *Languages of Class. Studies in English working class history 1832–1982* (Cambridge, 1983), pp.90–178.
15. Mark Bevir, 'The British Social Democratic Federation 1880–1885. From O'Brienism to Marxism', *International Review of Social History*, 37, 1992, pp.207–29; Mark Bevir, 'Republicanism, socialism, and democracy in Britain. The origins of the radical left', *Journal of Social History* 34, 2000, pp.315–68.

16. See, e.g., H.M. Hyndman, *The Economics of Socialism* (London, 1896); William Morris and Ernest Bax, *Socialism. Its Growth and Outcome* (London, 1893).
17. H.M. Hyndman, 'The dawn of a revolutionary epoch', *Nineteenth Century*, 9, 1881, p.17.
18. H.M. Hyndman, *The Text Book of Democracy. England for all* (London, 1881), p.31.
19. *Justice*, 14 June 1884.
20. William Morris, *News from Nowhere*, in The *Collected Works of William Morris* (London, 1910–15), vol.16.
21. Joseph White, *Tom Mann* (Manchester, 1991).
22. On the Fabians and their intellectual ancestry, see Norman and Jean MacKenzie, *The First Fabians* (London, 1977); Willard Wolfe, *From Radicalism to Socialism* (New Haven, CN, 1975).
23. Mark Bevir, 'Fabianism and the theory of rent', *History of Political Thought*, 10, 1989, pp.313–27.
24. Sidney Webb, 'English progress towards social democracy', *Fabian Tract*, no. 15, 1892, p.5.
25. Sidney and Beatrice Webb, *Industrial Democracy* (London, 1902), esp. pp.863–72.
26. At first Webb advocated the positivist solution of moralisation of the capitalist: see Sidney Webb, 'The economics of a positivist community', *Practical Socialist*, 1, 1886, pp.37–9. Before long, however, he rejected this solution on the grounds that it would not address the inefficiencies of the free market: see Sidney Webb, 'Rome. A sermon in sociology', *Our Corner*, 12, 1888, pp.53–60, 79–89.
27. George Bernard Shaw, 'The economic', in G. Shaw (ed.), *Fabian Essays in Socialism* (London, 1890), p.27.
28. Shaw, 'The transition to social democracy', in *Essays*, p.182.
29. On the importance of Carlyle and Ruskin for ethical socialism, see Stanley Pierson, *Marxism and the Origins of British Socialism* (Ithaca, NY, 1973); and Mendilow, *Romantic Tradition*. On ethical socialism, also see Stephen Yeo, 'A new life. The religion of socialism in Britain, 1883–96', *History Workshop*, 4, 1977, pp. 5–56.
30. Edward Carpenter, *The Art of Creation* (London, 1904), p.50.
31. Edward Carpenter, 'The value of the value theory', *To-day*, 11, 1989, pp.22–30.
32. Wilfrid Richmond, *Christian Economics* (London, 1888), p. 25.
33. Frank Trentmann, 'Wealth versus Welfare. The British left between Free Trade and National Political Economy before the First World War', *Historical Research*, 70, 1997, pp. 70–98.
34. Edward Carpenter, *Angel's Wings* (London, 1898), p.226.
35. E.g. 'Preferential Dealing', in Christian Social Union (Oxford Branch), Leaflets, Bodleian Library, Oxford.
36. Edward Carpenter, 'Transitions to freedom', in *Forecasts of the Coming Century*, ed. E. Carpenter (Manchester, 1897), pp.174–92.
37. *Commonweal*, 5 December 1891.
38. Charles Gore, *Strikes and Lock-Outs. The way out* (London, 1926), p.12.
39. Of course, the divisions were never as clear-cut as this suggests. So, for example, Sydney Olivier, a Fabian, held views remarkably close to those described as ethi-

cal socialism: see Sydney Olivier, *Sydney Olivier: Letters and Selected Writings*, ed., M. Olivier (London, 1948). Likewise, many of the early socialists changed their beliefs somewhat, often under one another's influence. So, for example, the Webbs and Carpenter briefly showed signs of being influenced by syndicalism: see Sidney and Beatrice Webb, *A Constitution for the Socialist Commonwealth of Great Britain* (London, 1920); Edward Carpenter, *Towards Industrial Freedom* (London, 1917).

40. Philip Snowden, *Socialism and Syndicalism* (London, 1913), p.84.
41. Ramsay MacDonald, *The Zollverein and British Industry* (London, 1903), p.163.
42. Snowden, *Socialism and Syndicalism*, p.117.
43. E.g. Ramsay MacDonald, 'Socialism', in B. Barker (ed.), *Ramsay MacDonald's Political Writings* (London, 1972).
44. Philip Snowden, 'The socialist budget 1907', in J. Hardie (ed.), *From Socialism to Serfdom* (Hassocks, 1974), p.7.
45. Ramsay MacDonald, *Socialism and Society* (London, 1905), p.70.
46. R.J. Holton, *British Syndicalism, 1900–14. Myths and realities* (London, 1976). On Connolly's political thought, see David Howell, *A Lost Left* (Manchester, 1986).
47. On socialist debates about the nature and role of democracy, see Logie Barrow and Ian Bullock, *Democratic Ideas and the British Labour Movement, 1880–1914* (Cambridge, 1996).
48. A.J. Penty, *The Restoration of the Gild System* (London, 1906). For discussion of the movement, see S.T. Glass, *The Responsible Society: The ideas of the English guild socialists* (London, 1966).
49. Penty, *Restoration*, p.57.
50. Once again, of course, the division was not as clear-cut as this suggests. So, e.g., Orage and Hobson were themselves members of the Fabian Society, albeit part of an internal opposition to Shaw and the Webbs; while the leading figures in the Labour Party, including MacDonald, were influenced at times by doctrines such as syndicalism. See Ramsay MacDonald, *Socialism. Critical and constructive* (London, 1921).
51. A.W. Wright, *G.D.H. Cole and socialist democracy* (Oxford, 1979); Michael Newman, *Harold Laski: A political biography* (Basingstoke, 1993).
52. Cf. Frank Trentmann, 'The strange death of free trade: The erosion of 'Liberal consensus' in Great Britain, c. 1903–1932', in E. Biagini (ed.), *Citizenship and Community* (Cambridge, 1996), pp.219–50.
53. J.A. Hobson and A.F. Mummery, *The Physiology of Industry* (London, 1889); Alfred Marshall, *Principles of Economics* (London, 1961).
54. Ramsay MacDonald, *Socialism after the War* (London, 1918), p.8.
55. David Green, *Reinventing Civil Society. The rediscovery of welfare without politics* (London, 1993); David Green, *Community without Politics. A market approach to welfare reform* (London, 1996).
56. Paul Hirst (ed.), *The Pluralist Theory of the State. Selected writings of G.D.H. Cole, J.N. Figgis, and H.J. Laski* (London, 1989); Paul Hirst, Associative Democracy. *New forms of economic and social governance* (Cambridge, 1994); Paul Hirst, *From Statism to Pluralism. Democracy, civil society, and global politics* (London, 1997).

Pessimism of the Intellect?
The *New Left Review* and the 'conjuncture of 1989'

Duncan Thompson

Forty years and 238 issues after its first appearance in 1960 one of the foremost Marxist journals in the English language, the *New Left Review*, marked the new century by commencing a new series with *NLR* (II) 1, January/February 2000. Although billed as a 'new *New Left Review*'[1] anyone expecting a statement of new political direction will be disappointed. This new series coincided with Perry Anderson's return as editor. Anderson judges that the journal, as it enters its fifth decade, where its life must be extended 'beyond the conditions' and 'generations that gave rise to' it, but the shape and direction of any such 'overhaul' is left curiously in the air: the 'transition to another style of review', Anderson writes, is 'not to be achieved overnight', cautioning that his editorial launching the new series is but 'a personal—and therefore provisional—statement'.[2] A rousing manifesto of the tasks of the journal and, more widely, a New Left politics, it is not.

The uncertainty of the project that will define the new series is a direct reflection of the *Review*'s reading of what Anderson calls the 'conjuncture of 1989'; namely, 'the virtually uncontested consolidation, and universal diffusion, of neo-liberalism'.[3] Even under notionally centre-left 'third way' governments of the Clinton–Blair type, the 'hard core of government policies remains further pursuit of the Reagan–Thatcher legacy…now carefully surrounded with subsidiary concessions and softer rhetoric', the combined effect of which, 'currently being diffused throughout Europe, is to suppress the conflictual potential of the pioneering regimes of the radical right, and kill off opposition to neo-liberal hegemony more completely'.[4] Thus, in Anderson's estimate, for 'the first time since the Reformation, there are no longer any significant oppositions—that is, systemic rival outlooks—within the thought-world of the West'.[5]

If the principal response of the erstwhile Left has been one of 'accommodation' to the triumph of capitalism, Anderson warns against what he describes as the politics of 'consolation', the search for 'silver linings', inducing 'a propensity to over-estimate the significance of contrary processes, to invest inappropriate agencies with disinterested potentials, to nourish illusions in imaginary forces'.[6] Instead, Anderson advocates for the *NLR* an 'uncompromising realism', 'refusing any accommodation with the ruling system, and rejecting every piety and euphemism that would understate its power'.[7] In a footnote Anderson identifies a third response on the Left; namely, 'resignation': 'a lucid recognition of the nature and triumph of the system, without either adaptation or self-deception, but also without any belief in the chance of an alternative to it'.[8] Although a 'bitter conclusion', and one 'rarely articulated as a public position',[9] we may speculate that this is perhaps, at least privately, the perspective with which Anderson feels the greatest affinity.

What is missing from Anderson's editorial—consistent with the general reticence of the second New Left concerning its own evolution—is any critical reflection upon the *Review*'s past. It is a history that, in contrast to that of the first New Left, is curiously unexplored, for neither accounts of their past involvement in the *NLR*, nor critical reflections upon the journal's history, have been forthcoming from anyone intimately involved in the post–1962 *Review*. Whilst of intrinsic interest in itself it is, moreover, a history that is central to understanding the *Review*'s reading of, and response to, the 'conjuncture of 1989', and thus its ability or otherwise to illuminate the terrain on which we must contest capitalism at the beginning of the twenty-first century.

The 'second' New Left

When Anderson and others inherited the *New Left Review* on the dissolution of the first New Left (Edward Thompson, Stuart Hall, Raymond Williams, *et al.*) in 1962, they were largely undaunted by the disappearance of the New Left as a political movement, and showed little interest in seeking to resurrect it. Writing in the *Review* in 1965, Anderson reflected that 'the hope of becoming a major political movement haunted' the first New Left, 'and ended by dissipating its initial assets'.[10] Henceforth, accordingly, the *Review*'s focus was the '[t]heoretical and intellectual work…sacrificed' by the first New Left 'for a mobilising role which perpetually escaped it'.[11] Its model was Sartre and de Beauvoir's *Les Temps Modernes*.[12] Thus, in a critique as early as 1964, Peter Sedgwick identified in Anderson and his closest associates a 'new New Left', 'rootless' and 'Olympian' in character.[13]

Significant differences between the two New Lefts there certainly were, though initially these were arguably more of style and temperament than political substance. The first New Left's focus was more immediate (even managing, for instance, to produce a four-page daily bulletin for delegates at Labour's 1960 Scarborough conference), as were its expectations: in Thompson's impatient diagnosis Britain was 'over-ripe' for socialism. After Thompson relinquished control, the *New Left Review*'s principal preoccupations continued to be popular culture and the recovery of working-class history 'from below' (in, for example, the work of the Centre for Contemporary Cultural Studies and the History Workshop). By contrast, as Gregory Elliott has argued, the second New Left thought in terms of 'epochs and continents';[14] was determined to see Britain, in some sense, 'as a foreign country';[15] and was committed to the importation and naturalisation of continental Marxism in a bid to fill the perceived 'absent centre' at the heart of British intellectual culture. It was thus altogether more intellectual and theoretical in register.

The sharp exchange with Edward Thompson in 1965–6 over the heterodox interpretation of modern British history offered in the 'Nairn-Anderson theses' served very publicly to demarcate the emergence of a 'new' or second New Left distinct from its forbears—though it is hard to avoid the conclusion that the intemperance of these polemics was in large part the consequence of a residual bitterness on Thompson's part, and a defensiveness on Anderson's, concerning the change in editorial control of the *Review*. At this stage, the second New Left, like the first, was committed to reformism, and Ian Birchall, writing in 1981, concluded that whilst the change in editorial control marked 'a significant shift in style and personnel', 'as far as politics was concerned there was no clear break'.[16] In this period, the second New Left advocated a proto-Eurocommunist policy of 'presence' and a strategy of structural reform. In 'Problems of Socialist Strategy' (1965), for example, Anderson counterposed a Gramscian war of position in civil society to both Leninist and social democratic fixation on the state, arguing that Leninism has 'meaning' only 'in backward, inchoate societies, dominated by scarcity and integrated only by the state,'[17] whereas 'in western Europe…capitalist hegemony is first and foremost entrenched in civil society, and must be beaten there'.[18] Anderson later critically reflected that such a reading of Gramsci exhibited the 'illusions of Left Social-Democracy'.[19]

Revolutionary expectations

In terms of substantive political reorientation, the real break came in 1968—as much a discontinuity within the career of the second New Left as a break between it and the first New Left. Whereas the latter, briefly regrouped around the *May Day Manifesto* and subsequent Convention of the

Left, continued to seek a third way between social democracy and communism, the events of that momentous revolutionary year radicalised, and effectively refounded, the second New Left. Above all, the French May was seminal, for it appeared to herald the 'return of the repressed' to the West.[20] The 'idea of the actuality of socialist revolution' reflected the editorial collective, looking back on the May Events in the one-hundredth issue of the *Review* in 1977, 'transformed political consciousness throughout the capitalist world'.[21] So far as one could judge from the *New Left Review*, the question of the transition to socialism in one or more of the advanced capitalist countries remained firmly on the political agenda for a decade or more.

Judging, in the new militant temper of the times, that the 'intellectual course' of Western Marxism—the product of defeat and the long separation of theory from revolutionary practice—had 'probably already been run',[22] the *Review* initially oriented itself towards Maoism and its western European offshoot, student revolutionism. Maoism was judged the theory of a genuine revolutionary practice, superior in important respects to Lenin, no less.[23] Thus, as it later acknowledged, the *Review* 'slid towards an uncritical substitution of China for Russia in its…political orientation', in which the 'record of the Chinese Revolution…functioned as a kind of absolution for the disasters of the Russian Revolution'.[24] Meanwhile, in June 1968 the *NLR* 'collectively participated as a group' in the founding conference of the Revolutionary Socialist Students' Federation,[25] whose eleven-point manifesto, committed 'to the revolutionary overthrow of capitalism and imperialism and its replacement by workers power',[26] was reprinted in full in the *Review*.

However, somewhat disabused of the limitations of student politics and illusions in Maoism, the *Review* gravitated, in a circuitous fashion, towards Trotskyism. In the immediate context of 1968, the *NLR* dismissed Trotskyism as having remained imprisoned in the experience of the October Revolution;[27] in Nairn's account, the Trotskyites 'remained the guardians of the flame, in a world that would not catch fire':[28] a 'profoundly conservative' task.[29] It was via 'a new debate on the twenties'[30] that the *Review* was first nudged in the direction of Trotskyism: an exchange on Trotsky's legacy initiated by Nicolas Krassó—a pupil of Lukács who had left Hungary in 1956, and a recent recruit to the editorial committee—and rejoined by Ernest Mandel. It was to Mandel's second reply, published in 1969, that the *Review* itself attributed orientation of the editorial collective in the direction of the Fourth International[31]—although unambiguous public endorsement of Trotskyism as 'one of the central elements for any renaissance of revolutionary Marxism' tradition was not made until 1976, in Anderson's *Considerations on Western Marxism*. But if Trotskyism was equally 'subject to the ultimate dictates of the long epoch of historical defeat for the working class in the West', did its legacy really make a 'polar contrast' to that of Western Marxism?[32] If, through its long divorce from revolutionary practice, Western Marxism became immersed in philosophical abstractions, the Trotskyist response involved its own penalties, not least a certain conservatism: '[t]he preservation of classical doctrines took priority over their development. Triumphalism in the cause of the working class, and catastrophism in the analysis of capitalism, asserted more by will than by intellect, were to be the typical vices of this tradition in its routine forms'.[33] Moreover, Anderson conceded, Trotskyism had yet to resolve 'the formidable scientific problems posed to the socialist movement' by the question of revolutionary strategy in the West.[34] Fully aware of Trotskyism's evident weaknesses, Anderson's affiliation was more forthright than his reservations warranted.

Whatever the merits or costs of this orientation, there seems to be no doubt that in the 1970s the *Review* developed a strong identity on the basis, in its own estimate, 'of an open and critical revolutionary Marxism'. In part, this identity derived from an organisational style that matched its politics— the assimilation of 'certain features of the modus operandi of a semi clandestine revolutionary organisation'—and effectively fashioned a collective *New Left Review persona*.[35]

Commercially too it was a success: the *Review* recorded its first annual surplus in 1967.[36] Benefiting from the rapid expansion of higher education since the 1960s, the *NLR* found a ready audience in a growing and radicalised academia. That there was a ready reception for classical and western Marxism is witnessed by both the collaboration with mainstream publisher Penguin Books in producing the Pelican Marx Library under the general editorship of Quintin Hoare, and the success of the *Review*'s own publishing imprint, New Left Books (now Verso), launched in 1970 (in Edward Thompson's caustic aside, 'import agencies' for continental Marxism[37]).

The *Trotskysant* complexion of the *NLR*'s editorial collective was strengthened both by the resignations of Ben Brewster and David Fernbach over editorial criticism of China in 1971, and the apparent inactivity of members at odds with the new orientation. Of the editorial committee's seven identifiably active members in the mid-1970s, three were members of the International Marxist Group (IMG), the British section of the Fourth International. Ernest Mandel, a leading figure in the Fourth International, became a major contributor to the *Review*[38] and his *Revolutionary Marxism*

Today, published by New Left Books in 1979 could be regarded as a manifesto of the Fourth International. However, whilst the '*coupure* of May' had led to the revolutionary reorientation of the *Review*, it left unchanged the second New Left's collective character trait from its birth: its Olympianism and high intellectualism.

Misreading the moment of 1968

The *Review* was not mistaken in its judgement concerning the prospects of a revolutionary transition to socialism in one or more of the advanced capitalist countries (southern Europe being identified as the potential weak link in the chain of metropolitan capital in the years after 1968)—it was a view shared across the political spectrum, by hopeful and fearful commentators alike. But what is most revealing about the orientation of the *NLR* is its commitment to the paradigm of 1917 and an excavation of the debates of the 1920s—'the last great strategic debate in the European workers' movement' on the development of a 'revolutionary strategy in metropolitan capitalism that…had any direct contact with the masses'[39]—and its failure to address the emergence of a 'post-affluence' socialist politics and the libertarian socialist agenda tabled by the events of 1968 and after in the development of a genuinely contemporary revolutionary politics, despite the fact, for example, that the IMG was itself 'heavily influenced by the antibureaucratic thrust of the women's movement, student radicalism, community politics, the squatters' and claimants' movements'.[40] Today, it is this agenda that constitutes the basis for an anti-capitalist, 'Red–Green' politics in the advanced capitalist countries. The *Review* would not have had to look far to discover the resources for such an engagement. Although Juliet Mitchell, according to Anna Coote and Beatrix Campbell the 'first major exponent of socialist feminism' in Britain,[41] remained on the editorial committee until 1983, the *Review* gave little space to such wider arguments and others went unrepresented—see, for example, the contents of the weekly newspaper *Seven Days* (1971–2), a collaborative venture involving individuals associated with the Women's Liberation Workshop, *Black Dwarf, Idiot International*, and Gay Liberation. The women's movement featured prominently in *Seven Days*, whose coverage ranged from mental health issues to the commune movement, from 'kids' lib' to Bloody Sunday in Derry.

In the event the political defeats of the 1970s multiplied, illustrating 'a spectrum of different types of blockage or error': from the 'fawning accommodation' of the PCI and the electoral misadventures of the PCF, to the bureaucratic 'sectarian putschism' of the Portuguese Communist Party[42]—

compounded more significantly still by the failure of the Fourth International in Portugal, where 'arguably the best single chance of a socialist revolution in Western Europe...was spectacularly missed'.[43] The strategic debate in the pages of the *Review* in this period was an energetic one, pitting Left Eurocommunists such as Claudin and Poulantzas against revolutionary Marxists such as Mandel and Henri Weber. However, it was also to prove inconclusive. Despite its revolutionary affiliation, the *Review* expressed a certain equivocation, unwilling, or perhaps unable, to adjudicate on the debate. An editorial report remarked that 'favourable [treatment] significantly outweighed critical treatment of Eurocommunism', while what criticism there was tended to reiterate 'classical tenets', rather than develop 'new revolutionary strategies'.[44] As early as 1978 Anderson was voicing his disappointment at the failure of the Fourth International to respond convincingly to the strategic impasse.[45]

Even from the outset of its revolutionary orientation in 1968, the *Review* had accepted that a revolutionary strategy appropriate to the conditions of the advanced liberal capitalist countries had yet to be formulated. But, having firmly situated itself within the revolutionary tradition of 1917,[46] an appropriate socialist strategy, wrote Anderson in 1983, remained 'the Sphinx facing Marxism in the West'.[47] Whereas in 1976 Anderson had maintained that Trotskyism might provide 'one of the central elements for any renaissance of revolutionary Marxism',[48] by 1983 he was compelled to acknowledge that 'the promise it contained' had not been 'fulfilled'.[49] The Trotskyist tradition had failed to provide a 'scenario for defeating capitalism in the West'—a 'blockage', he argued, which 'stemmed from too close an imaginative adherence to the paradigm of the October Revolution'.[50] It is a criticism that might be applied equally to the *Review* itself.

Facing the Sphinx

Meanwhile, the period of revolutionary expectations heralded by the moment of 1968 had passed. The *Review*'s Decennial Report in 1974 had concluded that the 'chances of the Left are now much greater than at any time since the start of the Cold War, in the advanced and ex-colonial countries alike'.[51] However, surveying global prospects six years later, the *NLR* conceded that '[n]o such confidence is possible in 1980'.[52] The decade of revolutionary expectations, opened in Europe on the streets of Paris in May 1968, had come to an end. 'The historical defeat of the European labour movement in these years was a momentous one', judged the *Review*, 'quelling ...any short-range prospect of progress towards socialism in this central zone of the imperialist world'.[53] The terms of the new conjuncture, by contrast, were to be set by a sustained ideological and political offensive by an invigorated 'new Right'.

The *Review* had provided little coverage of domestic politics since the late 1960s—writing in 1977, Geoff Hodgson judged that the *NLR* had become the 'lost sheep of the labour movement',[54] too remote from the institutions of organised labour and the problems confronting any realistic political strategy for the attainment of socialism in British; similar critiques were penned by Mike Rustin and Donald Sassoon.[55] In 1980, however, the *Review* advocated a conscious 'reanchorage in Britain'[56] which initially reflected a new-found confidence in the health of Anglo-Marxism and the potential of the left-wing insurgency within the Labour Party. But reanchorage was also, at least implicitly, a recognition that the *Review*'s search since 1968 for an answer to the strategic questions facing a New Left politics in the West within the canon of classical revolutionary Marxism had proved unavailing. This was a potentially fruitful moment in the career of the second New Left, promising to focus its attentions upon the development of a genuinely contemporary revolutionary politics.

Anderson was soon to recognise that the challenge of the issues raised by gender, ecology and war 'have now become unevadable'.[57] While judging that the peace movement, bringing hundreds of thousands onto the streets of western Europe in protest, represented perhaps 'the greatest hope in European politics of the last few years',[58] it was the *Review*'s engagement with the question of feminism and the women's movement that was to prove central to its evolution. The *Review* had largely ignored the women's liberation movement since its inception in 1970; an intervention by a member of the *NLR* collective—by Branka Magas in 1971—concluded that socialism was a precondition for women's liberation and hence asserted the primacy of class politics.[59] However, the 1980 editorial report did suggest that the *Review* 'should...have a conscious programme for the integration of gender into class debates within the socialist culture it seeks to develop', adding that a 'sexual—as well as ecological—politics will clearly be salient parts of any late 20th-century socialism'.[60]

Nonetheless, Anderson considered that the very universality of the appeal of the women's, peace, and Green movements provided no specific leverage to effect the far-reaching social transformation necessary to the resolution of the problems they raised, a transformation that could only be achieved by the overthrow of capitalism.[61] Although the *Review* recognised the value of the pre-figurative and utopian dimension to these new movements—arguing that the 'long-separated traditions' of 'utopian' and 'scientific' socialism must 'be rejoined...today'[62]—it maintained that socialism still needed a perspective indicating 'particular agencies and strategies for its realisation'.[63] The 'decisive advance' of Marxism, Anderson argued, had been to identify 'the site of a particular social agency...as the Archimedean point from which the old order could be overturned—the structural position occupied by the industrial working class created by the advent of capitalism'.[64] But while there were 'structural reasons why the classical labour movement still remains the most steadfast component of an anti-capitalist politics', it was the new social movements, wrote Anderson, *et al.* in 1984, that 'have...in recent years often shown themselves superior to the workers' movement in terms of ideal–political imagination and immediate capacity for moral mobilisation'.[65] What was required was 'an alliance between the older labour movements and the anti-capitalist elements in the new social movements, which alone can secure the goals of each'[66]— in effect, a combination of social power and moral mobilisation, sustained by a 'concrete utopianism'. The *Review*'s public recognition of the limits of the classical revolutionary tradition, and its apparent willingness to engage with the utopian and pre-figurative themes raised by new social currents and forces, was potentially of great significance. The moment, however, was to be short-lived.

Retrenchment

It was soon evident that the crisis of socialist politics—attributable, Anderson has argued, to the recent defeats suffered by the Left and the 'double disappointment' in Maoism and Eurocommunism[67]—had escaped its Latin quarantine. At odds with this public expression of confidence in the health of Anglo-Marxism (see *In the Tracks of Historical Materialism*, 1983) an editorial report of late 1982 privately accepted that Britain and America had 'now also been infected by local variants of the continental virus',[68] expressed in Britain as a crisis of the labour movement and taking its cue from Hobsbawm's seminal work of 1978, *The Forward March of Labour Halted?*[69] Indeed, as early as 1981 Anderson was privately warning that in Britain the decomposition of Eurocommunism was threatening a similar rightward movement to that experienced in southern Europe.[70] As some on the Left, 'pink Professors and their even paler house-journals'[71] rallied to a moderating 'realism', the 1982 editorial report, while not wishing to 'warrant a retreat to the isolationism of the review in the past', suggested 'a greater measure of reserve towards our immediate environment'.[72] How far it was safe, in such a context, to pursue 'reanchorage' and venture from the *Review*'s previously self-imposed isolation was to prove problematic for the *NLR*. It may have also contributed to a sharp exchange within the editorial committee, which ultimately issued in the resignation of ten of its members (though only two active members, Anthony Barnett and Fred Halliday) at the end of 1983.

Plans to enlarge the editorial committee following the 1983 resignations went awry when four of the five women invited to join—Cathy Porter, Lynne Segal, Barbara Taylor and Hilary Wainwright—tabled demands which the editorial committee could not accept. The majority view of the *NLR* (Francis Mulhern, for one, dissented) was that the labour and women's movements had distinct goals. As its 1983 charter argued: 'Just as *NLR* is not a peace journal, but a socialist journal that supports the peace movement, so it is not a feminist journal but a socialist journal that supports the women's movement.' Having situated the working class, in Anderson's words, at the Archimedean point from which the old order could be overturned, what the *Review* sought was an alliance between the two movements. But Porter, Segal, Taylor and Wainwright countered that a gender-neutral workers' struggle was an insidious illusion since, in the first instance, it failed to challenge existing inequalities within the labour movement and organisations of the Left. They did not believe that feminism could be simply tacked on to existing socialist theory and political practice: it was not an alliance of feminism with socialism they sought, but a feminist reformulation of socialist politics. The editorial committee was enlarged early in 1984, a number of the new recruits included: Victoria Brittain, Patrick Camiller, Peter Dews, 'Oliver MacDonald' (Peter Gowan) and Ellen Wood.[73]

By 1985 the *Review* was writing that the current political scene was 'a much harsher one than anything the Left has known since the '30s'.[74] The domestic Left was in undisguised disarray: of its main detachments, the miners had been defeated, and left-wing local government either abolished or isolated and disowned by a rightward moving Labour leadership. In this new, and increasingly unfavourable conjuncture, it became apparent that the debate around *The Forward March of Labour Halted?*, 'at least so far as some of its participants were concerned', had 'acted to clear the ground for an increasingly outright repudiation of the very notion of an anti-capitalist working class'.[75] Far from seeking a combination between the labour movement and the 'new social movements', *Marxism Today*, main exemplar of the 'new revisionism', counterposed them. Significantly, Raphael Samuel, denouncing these 'Filofax Marxists' and 'Designer Socialists', contended that in counterposing 'the "new social forces" to the "pre-historic" ones represented by the trade unions', *Marxism Today* had 'tak[en] its cue from feminism'.[76] In championing the politics of the new social movements, the 'new revisionists' served to make them suspect in the eyes of the *NLR*. In any event, by the mid-1980s the peace movement was in visible decline, and the women's movement fragmented.

Nervous of the revisionist contagion, and by now wary of too radical a reformulation of socialist politics, the *Review*'s response to the new revisionists' coded assault upon socialism was a defence of class politics. In a keynote essay in the *Review*'s one hundred and fiftieth issue in 1985, Ralph Miliband (like Samuel, a key figure of the 'first' New Left) argued that the 'organised working class' remained the 'principal…"gravedigger" of capitalism', the 'indispensable "agency of historical change"'.[77] Other social forces had a role to play, but the structural location of the working class within capitalist production and reproduction meant that it was the only social actor with sufficient leverage to overturn capitalism. If 'the organised working class will refuse to do the job', Miliband concluded, 'then the job will not be done; and capitalist society will continue, generation after generation, as a conflict-ridden, growingly authoritarian and brutalised social system'.[78] Equally forceful interventions were made in the *Review* and elsewhere by members of the editorial collective, such as Geras, Mulhern, and Wood.[79] It was symptomatic of the defensiveness of its engagement with the new revisionism that the *Review* was more forthright in its reassertion of basic tenets of classical socialism, than in its resolution of the problems acknowledged to be confronting socialist strategy in the West.

The crisis of left-wing politics in Britain was due to no mere local, or temporarily unfavourable, turn of events: it affected the entire west-European Left, north and south, social democrat and communist alike. The failure of the French Left's projected 'rupture with capitalism' in 1981–2 set the boundaries for the reformist experience in neighbouring countries; thereafter 'Eurosocialism'—enthusiastically endorsing Atlanticism, the Cold War and anti-communism—embraced neo-liberal capitalist rationalisation: 'Reaganomics with a socialist gloss', as James Petras put it in the *NLR* in 1984.[80] In mapping the west-European Left in this period[81] the *Review* focused almost entirely on the principal parties of the centre Left; busy, in the *Review*'s words, 'dumping awkward commitments' and adjusting 'their sights downwards, confining themselves to ever more modest instalments of redistribution and promises to reduce unemployment, while having nothing to say about the organisation of production or the pattern of ownership'.[82] Despite heralding 'red-green' parties such as the Left Socialists in Norway as supplying 'a needed element of socialist renewal',[83] many anti-capitalist parties and movements were absent from the *Review*'s survey—indicative, perhaps, that it had abandoned its search for an answer to the question of revolutionary strategy in the west. Instead, the *Review* looked east.

The fall in the East

Central to the conjuncture of the 1980s was the West's calculated escalation of geo-political tension with the Soviet Union issuing, from late 1978, in a 'second' Cold War. Rejecting Edward Thompson's thesis that the 'second' Cold War was driven by its own 'exterminist' momentum, Fred Halliday countered that while the possession of nuclear weapons 'at once dramatise and endow' the conflict 'with infinitely greater risk', its 'bases lie elsewhere—above all in the conflict between capitalist and post-capitalist worlds'.[84] In Halliday's analysis, the origins of the renewed Cold War lay in a threefold right-wing offensive against the global post-war settlement, targeted at the domestic gains of the working class; at the USSR as a world power; and at the independence of the former colonial world. Counting fourteen 'revolutionary upheavals' in the Third World between 1974 and 1980,[85] Halliday judged that 'it is social revolution itself and the response to it which has triggered the counter-revolutionary drive that is so central to the Second Cold War'.[86] It was the West, 'precisely because it has the upper hand', that had taken 'the initiative in introducing a new level of competition which it believes will restore the primacy in world politics which recent developments have taken from it'.[87] In the same spirit the *NLR* was quick to recognise that the advent of the Second Cold War in 1978–9 'manifestly imposed new duties on the review'.[88] The *Review* was under no illusions as to what Halliday called the 'involuted and bureaucratic'[89] character of the 'socialism' on offer in the Soviet Union: its 1983 Charter condemned the communist states for exercising a 'repressive tutelage over the working population', denying them 'fundamental rights of self-expression and self-determination'.[90] However, in the climate of orchestrated 'Gulagism',[91] and the slippage of erstwhile leftists from anti-Stalinist to anti-communist and anti-socialist perspectives, a vigilant 'anti-anti-Sovietism'[92] (in Gregory Elliott's words) was deemed an unavoidable obligation.

Despite the further tarnishing of the image of 'actually existing socialism'—by, for example, Polish martial law, presidential shoot-outs in Kabul, the 'dementia'[93] of 'Democratic Kampuchea', and the outbreak of war between rival 'socialist' countries in Indo-China—the *Review* nonetheless judged that 'the Communist states' represented 'a historic progress over the capitalist or pre-capitalist societies that preceded them', and provided 'a vital bulwark against imperialism'; adding that the *Review*'s duty was to 'defend them…against every variety of capitalist attack, to which they are ceaselessly subject'.⁹⁴ Even North Korea, with an 'extraordinarily monolithic and regimented social order prostrated before the narcissistic cult of…[its] Communist monarch',⁹⁵ elicited a sober and sympathetic treatment in Jon Halliday's 1981 essay.⁹⁶ Moreover, while recognising that 'the unwelcome shocks suffered by the world imperialist system' in Vietnam, Angola, Ethiopia, South Yemen, and Afghanistan had all been 'facilitated or safeguarded by Soviet arms or assistance',⁹⁷ the *Review* disagreed with Trotsky's judgement that the Soviet Union was a counter-revolutionary force abroad: a 1978 editorial praised the progressive character of Soviet foreign policy, with specific reference to Vietnam and Afghanistan.⁹⁸

As the prospects of a breakthrough in the First World receded, the *Review* increasingly judged the prospects for socialism in terms of the global contest between East and West. In 1980 it accepted, confidentially, that it would have to bear 'with fortitude' the 'grim prospect' that the cause of socialism in the West might remain stalled until a democratic model proved viable in the East.⁹⁹ This said as much for the impasse of socialist strategy in the West as it did of the likelihood of democratisation in the Soviet Union. Events, however, were about to unfold at an unforeseen pace, and the ascension of Mikhail Gorbachev to the leadership of the CPSU in 1985 raised expectations of reform from within the ranks of the party bureaucracy. Affording 'historical priority to progress in the East over advance in the West'¹⁰⁰ was to prove decisive in determining the *Review*'s political trajectory as it navigated the 'crisis of socialism'. As Tariq Ali (who had joined the editorial committee in 1983) put it to Yuri Afanasyev in an interview in the *NLR* in 1988:

> Many of us who remain socialists in the West are beginning to regard the Soviet Union once again as a country of hope. If you succeed, it could help in the rebirth of mass socialism elsewhere in the world. In that sense the fight for a socialist democracy is important not just for you but for the whole world as well.¹⁰¹

Similar sentiments were echoed by the *Review* early in 1989, which considered that 'an alliance between the Western Left and socialist reform forces in the East could throw back the neo-liberal offensive of the past decade'.¹⁰² Substantial hopes were thus invested in a transition to socialist democracy in the East at a time when, on other fronts, West and South, prospects were at a premium, and thus the 'fall' of 1989–91 could not but have profound consequences for the *Review*'s geo-political perspective and its estimate of the prospects for socialism. The *NLR* had already privately contemplated, in 1980, the possibility of capitalist restoration in the East. It seemed 'historically implausible' that there would be no individual cases of restoration, 'however jolting the prospect. After all, the bourgeois revolutions were followed by a number of absolutist restorations, even if these did not prove durable in character—1660, 1815, 1824'.[103] Yugoslavia might be one such candidate for capitalist restoration, China 'possibly' another.[104]

The penalties of Olympianism

A certain 'super-theoreticism'[105] may have its place in an intellectual division of labour within the culture of the Left, but the lack of 'control' (through a closer relationship to its political constituency or readership) that comes with a detached intellectualism has its penalties, not least in strategic thinking.[106] The second New Left's search for a convincing political strategy was hampered both by its failure to shake off its early conviction that intellectual leadership had to come from outside the working class,[107] deflecting it from developing any organic links with either the labour movement or other progressive social forces, and by its privileging the task of transforming high intellectual culture, for whilst the undoubted growth of Marxism in Britain had, in Thompson's words, produced 'a mountain of thought', it had failed to give 'birth to one political mouse'.[108] Whilst the insights to be gained from a perspective that measures in terms of 'epochs and continents' are not to be doubted, the costs have been central to the *Review*'s evolution. The *NLR* was not mistaken in construing the events of 1968, chiefly the French May, as opening the prospect of a transition to socialism in one or more of the advanced capitalist countries. But unable to escape its romance with the moment of 1917, it did not engage with the libertarian socialist currents (or, indeed, a radicalised labour movement) that surfaced after 1968 and no *concrete* revolutionary analysis, comparable to Anderson's reformist 'Problems of Socialist Strategy' of 1965, was produced. Acknowledging the strategic impasse that had been reached at the end of the 1970s, the *Review*'s willingness then to engage with the British Left and the issues raised by, amongst others, the women's movement was a potentially fruitful moment. However, the moment was lost: an epidemic of defeatism on the Left induced the *Review* to retreat to isolation and, instead, everything was wagered, in a grand geo-political gesture, on the East.

The most recent attempt to engage directly with the domestic Left ended in 1993, when the addition of a cross-section of individuals to the editorial committee three years earlier led to a dispute over ownership and control of the journal which was followed by the resignation of nineteen of its members.[109] (The majority of the eight 'old guard' who remained—Anderson,

Tariq Ali, Blackburn, Brenner, Cockburn, Davis, Gowan and Sprinker—were based in North America, reinforcing the dislocation between the *Review* and any anchorage in the British left). The journal, of course, continues, and, while the *Review* has continued to provide excellent coverage of global affairs, the editorial project is not always easy to discern. If, as Anderson writes in launching the new series, the future trajectory of the *Review* is unclear, this is but a belated acknowledgment of an uncertainty that has been evident for a decade.

Suitably chastened by the events of 1989–91, and maintaining an Olympian perspective in preference to the closer scrutiny of, and engagement with, the admittedly small and fragmented opposition to the neo-liberal order on the ground (though certainly no smaller than the detachments of the Fourth International to which the *Review* was oriented in the 1970s), the *Review* began to articulate (without endorsing) a minimalist liberal-socialism—involving an acceptance of some key themes of the lately reviled new revisionism, and a quiet abandonment of its erstwhile revolutionary politics. In *After The Fall*, published by Verso in 1991, Blackburn, for example, now insisted that 'the Left must respect the complex structures of self-determination which the market embodies',[110] whilst the collection of essays led, significantly, with Norberto Bobbio, whose 'distinctive synthesis of liberalism and socialism'[111] had won Anderson's praise in the *NLR* in 1988;[112] in the new conjuncture, wrote Anderson, Bobbio had come 'into his own'.[113]

While a liberal-socialism may be justified in the immediate term as a rallying point upon an unfavourable terrain, the *Review*, given its precise advantage of thinking in terms of 'epochs and continents', might have been better placed than most to offer a bolder, longer-term perspective. Unwilling to connect with those social and political forces contesting global capital, the *Review*'s interventions in contemporary politics have been modest in scope. In 1991 Anderson wrote approvingly that Charter 88 had proved the 'liveliest recent movement within civil society'[114]—although it was the poll-tax rebellion, a far livelier movement, which could take no small credit for Thatcher's downfall. In 1992, in the *Review*'s first intervention in a British general election since 1964, Blackburn advocated tactical voting.[115] It is not enough to recognise, with Anderson and Camiller, that social democracy has 'lost its compass', '[t]rapped between a shifting social base and a contracting political horizon', where financial deregulation and international currency speculation have undermined its traditional Keynesian policy tools and the 'new tax aversion' has 'drastically narrowed' the 'limits of fiscal initiative'.[116] Social democratic management of capitalism was never what most of us meant by socialism, then or now. The 'new reality' is indeed 'a massive asymmetry between the international mobility and organisation of capital, and the dispersal and segmentation of labour, that has no historical precedent', and it may be that, for the present, the 'globalisation of capitalism', far from drawing 'the resistances to it together', has 'scattered and outflanked them', resulting in 'a reduction in social capacities to fight for an alternative to capitalism'.[117] The point, however, is to explore the basis upon which new coalitions within an internally divided global working class (broadly defined) can be built.

While we should endorse an uncompromising realism in preference to facile illusions in the prospects of radical social change, global capital is not invincible. If extraordinarily dynamic, it remains inherently unstable. Its greater reach merely multiplies the points at which it may break down and begin to unravel. If, in its new series, the *New Left Review* is unlikely to abandon the undoubted advantages of its Olympian perspective, engaging with those social and political movements that are actively contesting global capital in the task of making a New Left will help guard that a salutary pessimism of the intellect is leavened by an equally necessary optimism of the will.

Acknowledgment

This article draws heavily upon a recently completed PhD at Brighton University, and I would like to express my thanks to my supervisor Gregory Elliott for his support and encouragement throughout. No blame, of course, should attach to Gregory's name for my conclusions. In citing unpublished material, I have followed the convention established in Elliott's *Perry Anderson, The merciless laboratory of history* (Minneapolis and London, 1998), p.xvii; namely, quoting directly from documents that 'bear no signature and possess an institutional character', and paraphrasing from signed papers.

Notes

1. Full back page advertisement, *Red Pepper*, September 2000.
2. Perry Anderson, 'Renewals', *New Left Review* (II), 1, January/February 2000, p.6.
3. Ibid., p.10.
4. Ibid., p.11.
5. Ibid., p.17.
6. Ibid., pp.13–14.
7. Ibid., p.14.
8. Ibid., p.13.
9. Ibid.
10. Perry Anderson, 'The left in the fifties', *New Left Review*, 29, January/February 1965, p.16.
11. Ibid., p.17.

12. *NLR*, 'A Decennial Report', unpublished editorial document, 1974, p.6.
13. Peter Sedgwick, 'The two New Lefts', *International Socialism*, 17 August 1964, reprinted in David Widgery (ed.), *The Left in Britain 1956–68* (Harmondsworth, 1976), p.148.
14. A perspective Trotsky attributed to Lenin, and Gregory Elliott in turn to Perry Anderson ('Olympus mislaid? A profile of Perry Anderson', *Radical Philosophy*, no. 71, May/June 1995, p.5).
15. Ibid., p.7: pitting Thompson's 'messianic nationalism' and 'maundering populism' (Perry Anderson, 'Socialism and pseudo-empiricism', *New Left Review*, 35, January/February 1966, pp.34, 35) against Anderson and Nairn's 'national nihilism', what Thompson characterised as a preoccupation with the experience of 'Other Countries'. ('The peculiarities of the English', *Socialist Register 1965*, reprinted unexpurgated text in *The Poverty of Theory and Other Essays* (1978), London, 1980, p.37), and Richard Johnson as 'a rather self-indulgent Anglophobia' (Johnson, 'Barrington Moore, Perry Anderson and English social development' (1980), in Stuart Hall *et al.* (eds), *Culture, Media, Language*, London, 1984, p.61).
16. Ian Birchall, 'The autonomy of theory. A short history of *New Left Review*, *International Socialism*, no. 10, Winter 1980/81, p.60.
17. Perry Anderson, 'Problems of socialist strategy' in Perry Anderson and Robin Blackburn (eds), *Towards Socialism* (1965) (Ithaca, NY, 1966), p.228.
18. Ibid., p.244.
19. Perry Anderson, 'The antinomies of Antonio Gramsci', *New Left Review*, 100, November 1976/January 1977, p. 27.
20. Introduction, *New Left Review*, 52, November/December 1968, p.5.
21. 'Themes', *New Left Review*, 100, November 1976/January 1977, p.1.
22. Perry Anderson, *Considerations on Western Marxism* (1976), London, 1989, p.101.
23. *NLR*, 'Document A: Theory and Practice: The *Coupure* of May', unpublished editorial document, 1969, p.10.
24. 'A Decennial Report', p.32.
25. Ibid., p.39.
26. 'Revolutionary Socialist Students' Federation, Manifesto', *New Left Review*, 53, January/February 1969, p.21.
27. 'The *Coupure* of May', p.9.
28. Tom Nairn, 'Why it happened', in Angelo Quattrocchi and Tom Nairn, *The Beginning of the End. France, May 1968* (London, 1968), p.129.
29. Ibid., p.130.
30. 'Themes', *New Left Review*, 44, July/August 1967, p.2.
31. 'A Decennial Report', p.31.
32. Anderson, *Considerations on Western Marxism*, p.100.
33. Ibid., p.101.
34. Ibid., p.103.
35. *NLR*, '*NLR* 1975–1980', unpublished editorial document, 1980, p.4. The characterisation of the *Review*'s modus operandi is Gregory Elliott's in his *Perry*

Anderson. The merciless laboratory of history (Minneapolis and London, 1998), p.xvii.
36. 'A Decennial Report', p.23.
37. Edward Thompson, *The Poverty of Theory and Other Essays* (1978) (London, 1980), p.366.
38. By 1983 Mandel had contributed more to the *Review* than anyone apart from Anderson and Nairn: no less than 13 articles and 250 pages (*NLR*, 'NLR 1980–1983', unpublished editorial document, 1982: appendix p.xi). For identification of an '*aktiv*', see Elliott, *Perry Anderson*, p.111.
39. Anderson, 'Gramsci', p.78.
40. John Callaghan, *The Far Left in British Politics* (Oxford, 1987), p.159.
41. Anna Coote and Beatrix Campbell, *Sweet Freedom. The struggle for women's liberation* (London, 1982), p.17.
42. 'NLR 1975–1980', p.41.
43. Perry Anderson, 'Communist Party history' in Raphael Samuel (ed.), *People's History and Socialist Theory* (London, 1981), p.155. 'The Fourth International', wrote Anderson in 1983, had 'lost its way at the cross-roads of the Portuguese Revolution' (*In the Tracks of Historical Materialism*, London, 1983, p.80).
44. 'NLR 1975–1980', p.19.
45. Perry Anderson, 'The strategic option. Some questions' in André Liebach (ed.), *The Future of Socialism in Europe?*, Interuniversity Centre for European Studies, 1978, pp.27–8.
46. *NLR*, 'Charter', unpublished editorial document, 1983, p.4.
47. Anderson, *Historical Materialism*, p.80.
48. Anderson, *Considerations on Western Marxism*, p.100.
49. Anderson, *Historical Materialism*, p.79.
50. Ibid.
51. 'A Decennial Report', p.85.
52. 'NLR 1975–1980', p.33.
53. Ibid., p.40.
54. Geoff Hodgson, 'The antinomies of Perry Anderson' in Hodgson, *Socialism and Parliamentary Democracy* (Nottingham, 1977), p.137.
55. Michael Rustin, 'The New Left and the present crisis', *New Left Review*, 121, May/June 1980, pp.63–89; and Donald Sassoon, 'The Silences of *New Left Review*', *Politics and Power*, 3, London, 1981, pp.219–54.
56. 'NLR 1975–1980', p.54.
57. Anderson, *Historical Materialism*, p. 83.
58. 'Themes', *New Left Review*, 130, November/December 1981, p.1.
59. Branka Magas, 'Sex politics and class politics', *New Left Review*, 66, March/April 1971, pp.69–92.
60. 'NLR 1975–1980', p.66.
61. Anderson, *Historical Materialism*, pp.91–3.
62. *NLR* (ed.), *Exterminism and Cold War*, London, 1982, p.ix.
63. Ibid.
64. Anderson, *Historical Materialism*, p.94.

65. Perry Anderson, Fölker Fröbel, Jürgen Heinrichs and Otto Kreye, 'On some postulates of an anti-systemic policy in Western Europe', Starnberg Institute for the Study of Global Structures, Developments and Crises, 1984, pp.17, 18.
66. Ibid., p.18.
67. Anderson, *Historical Materialism*, p.76.
68. 'NLR 1980–1983', p.45.
69. Verso who published *The Forward March of Labour Halted?*, in association with *Marxism Today*, as a collection of essays in 1981.
70. Perry Anderson, 'A problem in defining the socialist society', unpublished document, 1981, p.1.
71. Tariq Ali, 'Labourism and the pink professors', in Tariq Ali and Ken Livingstone, *Who's Afraid of Margaret Thatcher?* (London, 1984), p.2.
72. 'NLR 1980–1983', pp. 51, 52.
73. *NLR*, 'Charter', p.10; see also Elliott, *Perry Anderson*, p.286, n.156, p.287, n.161.
74. 'Themes', *New Left Review*, 150, March/April 1985, p.1.
75. 'NLR 1980–1983', p.46.
76. Raphael Samuel, 'Class politics. The lost world of British communism, part three', *New Left Review*, 165, September/October 1987, pp. 76, 83, 90–1.
77. Ralph Miliband, 'The New Revisionism in Britain', *New Left Review*, 150, March/April 1985, p.13.
78. Ibid.
79. Norman Geras, 'Post-Marxism?', *New Left Review*, 163, May/June 1987, pp.40–82; Francis Mulhern, 'Towards 2000, or News From You-Know-Where', *New Left Review*, 148, November/December 1984, pp.5–30; and Ellen Wood, *The Retreat From Class. A new, 'true' socialism* (London, 1986).
80. James Petras, 'The rise and decline of Southern European socialism', *New Left Review*, 146, July/August 1984, p.42.
81. A series commenced in 1984 and collected and published by Verso a decade later: Perry Anderson and Patrick Camiller (eds), *Mapping the West European Left* (London and New York, 1994).
82. 'Themes', *New Left Review*, 165, September/October 1987, p.1.
83. 'Themes', *New Left Review*, 181, May/June 1990, p.2.
84. Fred Halliday, 'The sources of the New Cold War', in *NLR* (ed.), *Exterminism*, p.291.
85. Fred Halliday, *The Making of the Second Cold War* (1983) (second edition, London, 1986), p.92.
86. Ibid., p.82.
87. Ibid., p.45.
88. 'NLR 1975–1980', p.24.
89. Halliday, 'New Cold War', p.327.
90. *NLR*, 'Charter', p.5.
91. 'NLR 1975–1980', p.23.
92. Elliott, 'Olympus Mislaid?', p.13.
93. Perry Anderson, 'Trotsky's Interpretation of Stalinism', *New Left Review*, 139,

May/June 1983, p.57.
94. *NLR*, 'Charter', p.5.
95. 'Themes', *New Left Review*, 127, May/June 1981, p.2.
96. Jon Halliday, 'The North Korean enigma', *New Left Review*, 127, May/June 1981, pp.18–52.
97. 'Themes', *New Left Review*, 117, September/October 1979, p.1.
98. 'Themes', *New Left Review*, 110, July/August 1978, p.1. While the April 1978 coup that brought the 'People's Democratic Party of Afghanistan' to power was broadly welcomed (see Fred Halliday, 'Revolution in Afghanistan', *New Left Review*, 112, November/December 1978, pp.3–44), the direct intervention of Soviet forces in December 1979 was viewed with considerable disquiet, given the 'imperialist response' this would provoke (see Fred Halliday, 'War and Revolution in Afghanistan', *New Left Review*, 119, January/February 1980, pp.20–41).
99. '*NLR* 1975–1980', p.71.
100. Ibid.
101. 'Yuri Afanasyev on the 19th Conference of the CPSU' (interview), *New Left Review*, 171, September/October 1988, p. 86.
102. 'Themes', *New Left Review*, 175, May/June 1989, p.1.
103. '*NLR* 1975–1980', p.70.
104. Ibid.
105. Lin Chun, *The British New Left* (Edinburgh, 1993), p.xvi.
106. Paul Hirst considered 'its failure to establish any political or democratic relation to its own "constituency"' as one of the *Review*'s main weaknesses ('Anderson's Balance Sheet', in Paul Hirst, *Marxism and Historical Writing*, London, 1985, p.5). The establishment of readers' groups was one of the demands tabled by Barbara Taylor and her fellow feminists when invited to join the editorial committee in 1984 (letter from Porter, *et al.*, cited Elliott, *Perry Anderson*, p.286, n.156).
107. Because, wrote Anderson in 1965, 'the relationship between the working class and culture, decisive for its consciousness and ideology is *inevitably* mediated through intellectuals, the only full tenants of culture in a capitalist society'. ('Socialist strategy', p.241). Again, two years later, he was writing that 'intellectuals and petit bourgeois…alone can provide the essential *theory* of socialism'. (Perry Anderson, 'The limits and possibilities of trade-union action', in Robin Blackburn and Alexander Cockburn (eds), *The Incompatibles. Trade-union militancy and the consensus,* Harmondsworth, 1967, p.266).
108. Thompson, *Theory*, p.383.
109. New members had included Christopher Bertram, Paul Cammack, Diane Elson, Ken Hirschkop, Monty Johnstone, Deniz Kandiyoti, Doreen Massey, Robin Murray, Mike Rustin (previously on the editorial committee 1962–4), Kate Soper, Hilary Wainwright and Elizabeth Wilson.
110. Robin Blackburn, Preface to Blackburn (ed.), *After the Fall. The failure of communism and the future of socialism*, London and New York, 1991, p.xiv.

111. Perry Anderson, *A Zone of Engagement*, London and New York, 1992, p.xii.
112. Perry Anderson, 'The affinities of Norberto Bobbio', *New Left Review*, 170, July/August 1988, pp.3–36.
113. Anderson, *Zone*, p.xii.
114. Perry Anderson, 'The Light of Europe', in *English Questions*, London and New York, 1992, p.347.
115. Robin Blackburn, 'The ruins of Westminster', *New Left Review*, 191, January/February 1992, p.23.
116. Anderson and Camiller (eds), *Mapping the West European Left*, p.15.
117. Perry Anderson, 'The Ends of History', in *Zone*, p.366.

The Jarrow Crusade, the National Hunger March and the Labour Party in 1936
A re-appraisal

Matt Perry

> Why should a first-class piece of work like the Hunger March have been left to the initiative of unofficial members of the Party and to the Communists and the ILP? Consider what a mighty response the workers would have made if the whole machinery of the Labour Movement had been mobilised for the Hunger March and its attendant activities. *(Aneurin Bevan, 1936)*[1]

In 1936, two great demonstrations of the unemployed caught the national imagination. One was the National Hunger March, the last of several such marches organised by the National Unemployed Workers' Movement (NUWM) with its predominantly communist leadership. The other was the 'Jarrow Crusade', publicising the plight of one of the worst-hit towns of the depression and inseparably identified with Jarrow's Labour MP Ellen Wilkinson. Standard accounts of 1936 contrast the success of the Jarrow march with the frustration of the one organised by the NUWM. Chris Cook and John Stevenson, in *Britain in the Depression*, described the Jarrow Crusade as a 'publicity triumph' whilst NUWM demonstrations 'faded into obscurity'.[2] Harry Harmer contrasts communist disappointment with 'the simultaneous success of Jarrow'.[3] Andrew Thorpe stated that none of the hunger marchers 'achieved the publicity accorded to the 1936 Jarrow March.'[4] This view is based on the favourable press coverage attracted by the crusade. If we probe more deeply, however, it becomes clear that this conventional view is erroneous. Aneurin Bevan's words strikingly demonstrate the impression that the National Hunger March of 1936 made upon one contemporary witness, and a truer picture is far more complex. Moreover, the attitude of the Labour Party itself has also been the subject of some confusion. Ralph Hayburn, in an article published in 1983, stated that the Jarrow Crusade received official support from the Labour Party whilst the National Hunger March did not.[5] Paul Lennox, a hunger marcher in 1936, also expressed this view.[6] The present article seeks to offer a re-appraisal of the events of 1936 in the light of the full range of evidence which has now come to light.

The Jarrow Crusade and the hunger marches were born of the same desperate circumstances, differing only in detail. Moreover, the National Government and the Labour Party leadership reacted to them in broadly the same way. Nevertheless revisionist historians of the 1930s are quick to contrast them. If they are to be compared we encounter difficulties. By almost any measure, except press coverage, it is clear that the Jarrow Crusade did not overshadow the NUWM marches. In terms of the number of participants, the size of the petition, the monies collected and the scale of the reception demonstration, the hunger marches of the NUWM equalled or outdid the Jarrow Crusade.[7] Thus, there are a number of quantifiable aspects to the marches but these hardly address the real issues.

Despite the emphatic insistence by its leaders that the Jarrow Crusade was not a hunger march, a note of caution should be sounded when it is set against the work of the NUWM. The two cannot be viewed in isolation as it is doubtful whether the Jarrow hunger march would have been conceived without the precedents set by the NUWM. Ellen Wilkinson, who was identified with the left of the Labour Party and a former communist, sought advice from Wal Hannington, the NUWM leader, on the planning and organisation of the Jarrow march.[8] She stated that the Jarrow marchers viewed the hunger marchers not as competitors but as comrades, 'To them, these other marchers were a welcome sign that other men felt the same as they did, and they were kicking too'.[9] Harry McShane, who headed the Scottish contingent of the 1936 NUWM hunger march, echoed these sentiments, 'There was not rivalry between our march and hers [Ellen Wilkinson's]...when our march met her we exchanged speeches of support'.[10] Even in secret session the communist leadership stressed an unsectarian approach. Harry Pollitt told a Communist Party of Great Britain Central Committee meeting on 10 October 1936 of the need to mention the Jarrow Crusade during the campaign against the Unemployment Assistance Board (UAB) scales.[11] Indeed, Richard Croucher has uncovered the work of a group of travelling NUWM members who held meetings outside labour exchanges along the route of the Jarrow Crusade in order to raise a welcome from the local unemployed.[12]

Metropolitan Police files indicate that Hannington was frustrated that the Jarrow Crusade attracted more interest than his march. Based on this evidence, Harmer has suggested that Hannington believed the Jarrow Crusade to be more successful than the National Hunger March. This single quote of reported speech is the only evidence offered to justify the claim that he was 'jealous' of and 'frustrated' by the crusade.[13] We must remember that these words were recorded during a closed meeting of associates planning the reception of the hunger march. In public, the actions of Hannington and the NUWM were unsectarian towards the Jarrow Crusade. It should also be pointed out that this statement was made before the National Hunger March's successes were apparent: its massive reception demonstration, the House of Commons debating time, the ministerial delegation and the 'postponement' of UAB cuts. Although both marches were subjected to Special Branch surveillance and were officially denounced and discouraged, in the cabinet and amongst police chiefs, the NUWM march was taken much more seriously than the Crusade. When the cabinet discussed the three marches of September 1936, the NUWM march was its primary concern and the blind march and the Jarrow Crusade were only briefly mentioned in point seven of the cabinet conclusions on the subject. The National Hunger March was also subjected to greater scrutiny from the Metropolitan Police, as the size of their respective files demonstrates.[14]

However, a simplistic contrast between the respectable Jarrow Crusade and the threatening NUWM march would also be wide of the mark. After 1933 there had been a marked shift in the tone of the NUWM. The CPGB had adopted a united front strategy which sought, amongst other things, Communist Party affiliation to the Labour Party. NUWM circulars stressed that the hunger march petition was aimed specifically at middle-class professionals.[15] Thus, unlike its predecessors, the 1936 NUWM march courted respectable opinion. This time there were no police baton charges and public and press reaction was much more sympathetic than had previously been the case. Indeed, it received wider support from the labour movement and was sympathetically reported in the *Daily Herald* (which was busy at this time denouncing those confronting the fascists) and Clement Attlee, the leader of the Labour Party, spoke on the platform of the reception demonstration in Hyde Park.

Despite the rhetoric of the crusade's leaders, the notion that there was a sharp conflict between the organisations, participants or goals is not borne out by closer examination of the historical evidence. In fact the three marches of 1936 (the National Hunger March, the Jarrow Crusade and the blind marchers), especially the first two, were often perceived as a part of the same phenomenon.

'Do not help these men'

The Jarrow Crusade coincided with the Annual Labour Conference, held that year in Edinburgh, and was discussed in the session on 'Unemployment, malnutrition and the Special Areas'. National Executive Committee (NEC) member Barbara Gould's introductory statement completely ignored the efforts of the hunger marchers:

> It is more than time that this great Movement took up these questions as a whole…The Government has been very much cleverer than you have. They know when people are being half-starved. They know a half starved people do not revolt.. Let us join together on a great Crusade to stop the misery of millions starving in the midst of plenty.[16]

As the debate continued it grew increasingly polarised. Gould had called for a report on the depressed areas. Ellen Wilkinson, having come straight from the Jarrow Crusade, intervened: 'Have we not had enough reports? Is there a pore in the body of an unemployed man that has not been card-indexed? What are you going to do?' She condemned the Labour Party leadership for their inaction and their attitude to both hunger marches:

> You cannot expect men trapped in these distressed areas to stay there and starve because it is not convenient to have them coming to London. What has the National Council done? It has disapproved of it. What has gone out from the General Council ? Letters to the local areas in fact saying in the politest language, "Do not help these men."

Wilkinson denounced the 'black circulars' sent to trades councils and constituency Labour Parties to prevent support not only for the NUWM march, but also for the Jarrow Crusade. She also revealed that the NEC had not allowed a collection for the Jarrow marchers among the delegates.[17]

Some speakers attempted to defend the party's record. Lucy Middleton, who was parliamentary candidate for Sutton, Plymouth and the wife of the Labour Party's national secretary, suggested that the Jarrow MP should adopt a non-party approach that sought support from respectable folk, such as vicars and teachers. This was precisely the approach the crusade had taken. Middleton's criticism of Jarrow's march sharpened, and she suggested that the report would prove 'infinitely more important, infinitely more influential than sending hungry ill-clad men on a march to London'. Arthur Jenkins, speaking for the NEC, followed with a flimsy defence of Labour's record. First, he declared 'We, in House of Commons, have put up the best fight we know how in one of the most prolonged and sustained debates the House of Commons has ever experienced.' Secondly, Ernest Bevin had produced a report on job creation.[18]

Yet, the Labour Party's position with regard to the unemployed marches was more complex than the denunciation in Edinburgh would suggest. The Labour Party leadership had played no role in this campaign that halted the original implementation of the UAB scales in early 1935. However, many rank-and-file Labour Party members had participated in this dramatic success. A Labour Research Department pamphlet noted that:

In every town and village of the country, almost without exception, protest demonstrations were held. In spite of the use of the Police against the demonstrators, the power of the Government was not sufficient to still the popular agitation which its action had aroused.

The pamphlet confidently predicted further unrest, 'When the new scales come to be applied they will be met with a storm as great as met those of January 1935.'[19] In July 1936 the National Government announced plans to introduce the new scales the following November. Thus there was pressure on the Labour Party to take the lead in a new movement. The Labour leadership, both the NEC and the National Council of Labour (the NCL, which bridged the TUC General Council and the NEC), were also anxious about the unity campaign and feared that communist affiliation would be successful. In this context, although official support was not given to the march itself, a demonstration that would coincide with the hunger march's arrival in London was organised with sanction from the highest levels of the movement.

Labour's dilemma

Indeed, the Labour leadership had sought but failed to direct protest into safe and official channels. The National Council of Labour called a special conference on 20 July to protest at the new unemployment regulations. This was 'confined to organisations associated with the official Labour Movement'; in other words, the NUWM were excluded.[20] This conference resolved to 'aid the unemployed by bringing the utmost pressure to bear on the Government and Members of Parliament through demonstrations and letters of protest.' On 24 July the National Council of Labour mapped out the direction of the campaign. It proposed a letter to the Prime Minister, a series of demonstrations and conferences between 17 and 31 October, but it rejected a means test ballot and the boycott of advisory committees. It also objected to a march on London for the dubious reason that it would be 'inadvisable and costly'.[21]

Judging by the minutes of the CPGB's Central Committee, the Labour Party NEC and the NCL, this was far short of what some of the membership wanted. Hannington reported to the Communist Party central committee that at the TUC conference, held at Plymouth on 7–11 September, there existed a 'strong feeling amongst the delegates that the leadership was sidetracking the issue'.[22] The NCL was being repeatedly called upon 'to give a national lead'. On 24 September, whereas the NCL had proposed local demonstrations, the London Trades Council Executive Committee pressed the NCL for a national Hyde Park demonstration to take place on November 8.²³ By then, the NCL had also received a proposal from the South Wales Joint Committee for industrial action against the new regulations. A month later, the Durham Miners' Association forwarded a similar call to the NCL. In fact, London Trades Council twice debated a motion of censure of the NCL for rejecting the South Wales proposal of industrial action against the new regulations.²⁴ In such circumstances, the labour movement's leadership was under pressure to act and associate itself with the National Hunger March. Yet, they had never given official support to a hunger march and this U-turn would have set a dangerous precedent in relations with the communists. The Labour Party leadership therefore faced the dilemma of having to participate in, indeed, to lead, any popular manifestation of opposition to the new UAB scales without associating itself with the NUWM or the CPGB. Given the experience of unemployed protest the communists were likely to be at the forefront of that opposition.

The National Hunger March reaches London

The Hyde Park demonstration against the means test was supported by the NCL, London Trades Council, and the London Labour Party. On 7 October, Herbert Morrison, no less, informed the Metropolitan Police of the intention to stage this demonstration and the police were surprised when they subsequently discovered that it would receive the Hunger March.²⁵ That Morrison should be involved seems odd, for he was, 'the party's leading anti-communist'. Indeed, days before the Hyde Park demonstration at the Labour Conference, he was berating communists for physically confronting the fascists in the East End, setting forth proposals for the public order act, and speaking for the NEC against the united front.²⁶ Officially, the NEC and the NCL continued to ostracise the CPGB and the NUWM. Thus, the NCL commissioned a pamphlet in May 1936 entitled *British Labour and Communism* denouncing the CPGB and attempts at unity or affiliation. It proscribed the NUWM as 'subversive and unworthy of recognition', and denounced its exploitation of, 'the most helpless section of the Labour Movement as a force for antagonism, dissent and disruption.'²⁷ To square this circle, the NCL provided speakers to the Hyde Park demonstration but did so on the understanding that there would be no speakers, as they later reported, 'to whom no official objection could be taken. This understanding was not kept. Communist speakers appeared on most of the platforms and the gathering has been represented as evidence of the determination of the rank and file to force the policy of the United Front regardless of conference.'²⁸ This was not the understanding that London Labour Party representatives had given Hannington. The NUWM leader explained his negotiations with Wall of the London Labour Party to the central committee of the CPGB:

> I raised the question of there being speakers from the marchers themselves. Yes, he agreed, one speaker on each of the six platforms. This means 24 official labour speakers to six marchers. When I objected he agreed that this was the sort of thing that we should be able to sort out as time went on.[29]

In all, eleven Labour MPs, among them Clement Attlee, the leader of the Labour Party, Will Thorne and Aneurin Bevan, spoke at the demonstration. The Transport and General Workers were represented by Leslie Pearmaine and Bernard Sullivan and the South Wales Miners' Federation by the communist Arthur Horner, while the London Trades Council and the NCL also had platform speakers. In part, this reflected the degree to which certain sections of the Labour Party were 'circular-proof', as Ellen Wilkinson put it, or immune to the strictures against joint activity. The London Labour Party had a representative on the march reception committee. He was G.R. Strauss, Morrison's right-hand man. Hannington reported to the CPGB Central Committee that the National Hunger March had the backing of Lanarkshire, Edinburgh, and Aberdeen Trades Councils, amongst others, and in Nottinghamshire a joint committee had been set up between the Labour Party and the NUWM for organising the march.[30] But it was in Wales that co-operation was closest. The South Wales Miners' Federation formed a Council of Action with the Welsh Labour Party and the Welsh TUC to organise and support the Welsh hunger marchers. At the 4000-strong send-off demonstration in Newport, the leader of the Labour group on the council and three MPs spoke.[31] Despite its obvious success, the inclusion of the communist Arthur Horner in the Council of Action still caused consternation in the NCL. On the other hand, there were instances where trades councils toed the black circulars line, such as in Bath, with the South Wales hunger marchers, or in Chesterfield, with the Jarrow Crusade. In Sheffield, the Labour town council refused to support the hunger marchers and the Trades Council voted 46 to 34 to reject aid to the hunger marchers.[32] Sheffield Trades Council even sought clarification from the NEC about the official position on the hunger march. The NEC resolved to send them a 'friendly letter…intimating that the NEC had not been consulted regarding the march and could therefore accept no responsibility'.[33]

The 1936 National Hunger March had gained more official support than any other hunger march in the interwar period, including the Jarrow Crusade. The London Trades Council (LTC) described the National Hunger March Hyde

Park demonstration as 'a landmark in working-class history'. The LTC annual report written after questions were raised on the NCL about communist links with the National Hunger March talked of its 'whole-hearted support' for the unemployed hunger marchers (and no mention was made of the Jarrow Crusade). It noted that the LTC bona fide credentials had been granted to the London reception committee of the Hunger March but made no mention of the connection with the NUWM which would have contravened the 'black circulars'-for which eleven trades councils had been stripped of recognition the previous year.[34] The Jarrow Crusade made no such impact on the labour movement and left no trace in the minutes of the NEC or NCL.

The Labour leadership dealt with its dilemma by what might be termed an engineered confusion. Its attitude to the National Hunger March was contradictory and ambiguous. As we have seen, both hostility to, and support for, the National Hunger March was officially sanctioned. This deception was even extended to the Labour Party's dealings with the Metropolitan Police. Behind this ambiguity lay the party's divisions between the rank-and-file and the leadership and between left and right. Its stance appeased both left and right within the party. This division reached right to the top of the movement and explains Attlee's prominent role in proceedings. Thus, it is hard to believe that Attlee and Morrison saw eye to eye on these matters. Attlee's presentation of an NUWM petition to the Ministry of Labour a few months earlier had been criticised by Morrison on the NCL.[35] Attlee himself spoke to the crowds on 8 November and addressed the House of Commons on behalf of the hunger marchers later in the week which must have annoyed Morrison who was so centrally involved in the black circular policy. Unemployment was, as Attlee's biographers note, 'of all subjects closest to his heart' and a problem he spoke to throughout his career as a 'special interest': as mayor of Stepney, an area of high unemployment, he had come to national attention in November 1920 by leading the deputation of metropolitan Labour mayors to Downing Street over the issue; it was the subject of his maiden Commons speech in November 1922; he took over from Mosley in the second Labour Government as Duchy of Lancaster with responsibility for unemployment sitting on the Economic Advisory Council and voiced loyal criticism of MacDonald and Snowden within cabinet over their inaction in the face of mounting jobless totals until August 1931.[36] There was also a lingering personal edge to the differences with the Labour leadership. Attlee had thwarted Morrison's leadership bid in 1935.[37] The Labour leader was also a firm friend of Lansbury who in 1921 had broken the law over payments to the unemployed in Poplar. To Attlee's dismay, Morrison had viciously denounced Poplarism and the imprisoned Lansbury.

One gauge of the contemporary impact of the Jarrow Crusade and National Hunger March is their reception in the House of Commons. Although the government had put out a statement on the 15 October stating that it would not receive any marchers, the story of Jarrow was heard inside the House. On 4 November the two Jarrow petitions were presented in the house by Ellen Wilkinson and Sir Nicholas Gratton-Doyle, the Conservative MP for Newcastle North. That day there was a short period of questions about Jarrow. The government was asked how many resolutions of support for Jarrow it had received, it was also questioned about the possibility of naval contracts for the town and about the actions of the National Shipbuilders Securities Ltd. Government representatives responded that Jarrow was benefiting from the recovery in shipbuilding on the Tyne and that there would be no special naval orders for the town. On the following day, Willie Gallacher, the Communist MP for West Fife, asked whether the Jarrow and blind marchers would be received by the government. Further mention of Jarrow was made in a discussion on foreign affairs when Morgan Jones pointed out that 'there were many Jarrows in the country'; indeed, he suggested, 'the mining valleys of South Wales almost constitute one expansive Jarrow'.[38] Thus, the Jarrow marchers were discussed, albeit briefly, in the House of Commons.

The marchers' petition

The House of Commons also signalled disappointment for the Jarrow marchers as their petition had been presented in their absence. Ellen Wilkinson had telephoned the Metropolitan Police arranging for the men to be nowhere near parliament when the petition was received.[39] The Jarrow men were on a steamer trip on the Thames, paid for by Sir John Jarvis, the Conservative MP for Guildford and initiator of the Surrey Fund for the relief of Jarrow, as the petitions were being handed over in parliament. When they discovered that 'the crowning feature of their march' had taken place without their participation they were 'very disheartened'.[40] When the marchers later met up with the delegation of MPs in parliament, they heard that, as David Riley, the marshal of the crusade, put it, 'you have drawn a blank.' The Special Branch report told of their reaction:

> The temper of the men appeared to have been roused and suggestions were made that they should stage a stay-in strike and remain at the House of Commons until they were given a hearing. On receiving further advice, however, they were prevailed upon not to create a scene, and eventually returned to their billets.[41]

As a consequence of their desire to remain respectable and to avoid a scene in the House of Commons, the leaders of the Jarrow Crusade were forced into the position of colluding with the police to deceive the marchers.

That was not the end of the Commons airing of the marchers' concerns. On 9 November, in a debate of Special Areas legislation, the Minister of Labour, Ernest Brown, spent a considerable time conjuring with Hebburn and Jarrow's unemployment statistics. At one point, he omitted women and juveniles in an attempt to give the impression that unemployment in Jarrow was smaller than was commonly thought. He concluded that though the level of unemployment was 'bad' there had been a 'great improvement'.[42] But the longest debate on the 1936 hunger marchers took place on 11 November with the motion to allow representatives of the NUWM march to address the House of Commons. Clement Attlee himself proposed the motion. In contrast to the petition and brief oral questions that accompanied the Jarrow Crusade, a four-hour discussion ensued.[43] Curiously, the Parliamentary Labour Party (PLP) later reported its support for the hunger marchers to the NCL without disagreement, despite the dispute over speakers on the Hyde Park demonstration.[44]

The political momentum developed by the marches forced the government to retreat and the Minister of Labour received the NUWM marchers on 12 November.[45] Their leaders had been sent guidelines by the authorities ruling out a ministerial or prime ministerial hearing.[46] However, the cabinet had resolved that it could not prevent a ministerial interview if MPs were accompanied by a few constituents and if this was not considered a delegation.[47] This decision was to apply to all marches equally. The loophole only became apparent through the persistent pressure exerted by the NUWM march. Therefore, the Jarrow Crusade was not alone in gaining the attention of the House of Commons. Indeed, the NUWM march was more successful in terms of getting the House to discuss the issue of unemployment. Furthermore, it was the NUWM march and not the Jarrow Crusade that drew a ministerial interview.

The National Hunger March did gain concessions on its stated objective, the new UAB regulations. The government, fearing opposition, took an extremely cautious approach to the new scales. On 15 July 1936 the Ministry of Labour had ordered that the Standstill Act [which said that…] should not continue after 15 November 1936. But the new regulations were considerably less harsh than the initial UAB scales that had sparked such a furious response. Calculations for large families, rents, and earnings were made more generous. In addition, an 18-month period was allowed whereby any reduction in benefit could be balanced by a transitional provision.[48] At the meeting between the Hunger March delegation and the Minister of Labour, Ernest Brown, implementation of the new cuts was postponed for two months. The opposition was, however, calling not for postponement but suspension. The partial retreat caused considerable embarrassment and confusion for the government. On 18 November Lieutenant-Colonel Muir, speaking for the government, rejected the possibility that the new scales might be suspended. Later that day, the Prime Minister himself was asked by Aneurin Bevan whether the scales would be suspended.[49] Chamberlain refused to answer, claiming that he had not been notified of the question (which Bevan disputed). There were to be no immediate reductions in benefit and new regulations were phased in cautiously so that uniform national scales were only achieved in May 1938 over three years after the initial attempt. Though the government's circumspection cannot be attributed to the National Hunger March alone, it did provide a reminder of the débâcle of February 1935 and the prospect that such opposition might develop anew.

By contrast, the Jarrow Crusade was less successful. At the end of the crusade, David Riley publicly commented that widespread sympathy 'will compel the Government to act'. Likewise Ellen Wilkinson stated that a fire of sympathy had been lit that 'will not be put out by Ministerial cold water'.[50] However, as Jarrow council minutes six months later demonstrate, the crusade did not bring jobs: '... despite the measure of nation-wide support given to Jarrow in its appeal for work nothing yet has been done that has provided the necessary work, and, accordingly has HM Government any intention of providing the necessary assistance to resuscitate industry at this time or is it the Government's intention to continue declining assistance?'[51] The failure of the crusade to achieve its declared objectives is demonstrated by the fact that in December 1936 Joe Symonds and David Riley were proposing a second march though they were firmly defeated by the Mayor. Paddy Scullion, a Labour councillor and Jarrow marcher, proposed a second march again in November 1938. On the *Manchester Guardian* article about the second proposal in the Board of Trade's press cuttings, an official cynically wrote in the margin 'why not Consett, it's nearer?'.[52]

Ironically, days before the crusade's departure, and a considerable time after the government knew of its existence, the ministers of Health and Labour were arguing in cabinet for a rearmament factory, not in Jarrow, but in Merthyr Tydfil, because 'it would have marked an immediate effect upon the morale of the population, of whom large numbers are today giving up all hope and becoming all the more bitter as they see themselves destitute in the midst of returning prosperity in the country generally.'[53] The cabinet concurred judging the psychological and physical state of the unemployed in Merthyr to be 'seriously disquieting'. A rearmament factory was to be immediately considered.[54] There was no such discussion of Jarrow. Merthyr, unlike Jarrow, was renowned for its militancy and had been a centre of agitation in early 1935 against Part II of the Unemployment Assistance Act. It was here that miners passed resolutions in favour of industrial action against the act. Indeed, the threat of a miner's strike against company unionism in South Wales was hastily put to the top of the cabinet agenda on 2 September 1936, the very day of the cabinet's consideration of Merthyr Tydfil's plight. As for Jarrow, the persuasions of public opinion were ignored by cabinet and opportunities to make a special case for the Tyneside town passed by. On 4 November, the day the crusade's petition was presented to the House of Commons, the cabinet was discussing the location of a cordite factory at either distressed Gretna or Bishopton; and a fortnight later the allocation of £14 million of Admiralty contracts to distressed and special areas were discussed. In neither of these sessions was Jarrow considered seriously.[55] The moderation of the crusade may have suited the tastes of newspaper editors and journalists, but cabinet minutes suggest it had less of an impact on actual government decision-making.

Despite the claims to the contrary, the National Hunger March had much greater impact than the Jarrow Crusade on both the government and the labour movement; its press coverage, though more sparse than the Jarrow Crusade, was considerable and largely sympathetic.[56] Historical commentary on the Jarrow Crusade is founded on a fundamental error: Jarrow was not the most successful unemployed protest, nor did it attract the contemporary publicity to match its subsequent fame. The Jarrow Crusade did not exert the same pressure on the Labour Party leadership or the government as the National Hunger March. This was due, rather ironically, to the fact that it did not have the organisation and political network available to the NUWM and the CPGB, even though this was the very reasons that the Jarrow Crusade was heralded by most of the press. Sympathy for the crusade was considerable; but as one speaker at the Edinburgh Labour Party conference pointed out, 'sympathy does not make a noise in the frying pan.'

Notes

1. *The Socialist*, November 1936, quoted in B. Pimlott, *Labour and the Left in the 1930s* (Cambridge, 1977), p.93.
2. J. Stevenson and C. Cook, *Britain in the Depression. Society and politics 1929–39* (London, 1994), p.216.
3. H. Harmer, 'Failure of the communists. The National Unemployed Workers Movement', in A. Thorpe (ed.), *The Failure of Political Extremism in Britain* (Exeter, 1988), p.45.

4. A. Thorpe, *Britain in the Era of the Two World Wars* (London, 1994), p.175.
5. R. Hayburn, 'The NUWM 1921–36: a re-appraisal', *International Review of Social History*, vol.28, 1983, p.285.
6. I. MacDougall (ed.), *Voices of the Scottish Hunger Marches*, vol.2, 1991, p.328.
7. W. Hannington, *A Short History of the Unemployed* (London, 1940); *Daily Herald*, 9 November 1936; J. Jacobs, *Out of the Ghetto. My youth in the East End, communism and fascism 1919–39* (London, 1991), p.266; *Daily Worker*, 9 November 1936.
8. W. Hannington, *Never on our Knees* (London, 1967), pp.314–16.
9. E. Wilkinson, *The Town That Was Murdered* (London, 1939), p.202.
10. H. McShane, *No Mean Fighter* (London, 1978), pp.217–18.
11. Communist Party of Great Britain, *Central Committee Minutes*, 10 October 1936, NMLH.
12. R. Croucher, *We Refuse to Starve in Silence* (London, 1987), p.181.
13. Harmer, 'Failure', p.46.
14. CAB 24/264, c.p.256, PRO; MEPO:2/3053 and 2/3091(NUWM) & 2/3097 (Jarrow), PRO.
15. NUWM circulars, 6 and 25 March 1936, quoted in Harmer, 'Failure', p.45.
16. *Report of the Labour Party Conference, Edinburgh 1936* (London, 1936), pp.222–3.
17. HC 253 IJ: A.A. Kennie (secretary, Jarrow Labour Party and Trades Council) to J.S. Middleton (secretary, Labour Party), letter [requesting permission for a collection at conference], 30 September 1936, TUC Library.
18. *Report, Edinburgh 1936* (London, 1936), p.230.
19. Labour Research Department, *Standards of Starvation. Five years of government policy to the unemployed* (London, 1936), pp.12–15.
20. National Council of Labour, *Minutes and Papers*, 16 July 1936, NMLH.
21. National Council of Labour, *Minutes and Papers*, 24 July 1936, NMLH.
22. Communist Party of Great Britain, *Central Committee Minutes*, 10 October 1936, NMLH.
23. London Trades Council, *Executive Committee Minutes*, 24 September 1936, TUC library.
24. London Trades Council, *Meeting of Delegates Minutes*, 8 October 1936 and 12 November 1936, TUC Library.
25. MEPO: 2/3053 item 1H, PRO; B. Donouhue and G. Jones, *Herbert Morrison. A portrait of a politician* (London, 1973).
26. *Report, Edinburgh, 1936* (London, 1936), p.164.
27. National Joint Council, *British Labour and Communism* (London, 1936), p.6.
28. National Council of Labour, *TUC Report to NCL*, 24 November 1936, NMLH. Leading communists did argue that the Hyde Park rally showed the rank and file's desire for the affiliation campaign. See R.P. Dutt, *What Next for the Labour Party?* (London, 1936); J. Strachey, 'What the hunger marchers have done', in *The Daily Worker*, 17 November 1936.
29. Communist Party of Great Britain, *Central Committee Minutes*, 10 October 1936, NMLH.
30. *Minutes*, 10 October 1936, NMLH.

31. Ellen Wilkinson Papers, WI/07: *South Wales Argus*, 26 October 1936, NMLH.
32. *Sheffield Independant*, 21 October 1936.
33. Labour Party *NEC Minutes*, 25 November 1936, NMLH.
34. London Trades Council, *What the L.T.C. is Doing*, 77th Annual Report (London, 1936); A. Clinton, *Trade Union Rank and File. Trades Councils in Britain* (London, 1977), p.35.
35. National Council of Labour, *Minutes and Papers*, 26 May 1936, NMLH.
36. K. Harris, *Attlee* (London, 1982), p.111; T. Burridge, *Clement Attlee. A political biography* (London, 1985), pp.43–113.
37. F. Beckett, *Clem Attlee* (London, 1997), p.122.
38. House of Commons *Debates*, Fifth Series, 1936–7, vol.317, col.369, 5 November 1936.
39. MEPO 2/3097 minute sheet, PRO.
40. MEPO:2/3097 item 28A, PRO.
41. MEPO:2/3097 item 28A, PRO.
42. House of Commons *Debates*, Fifth Series, vol.317, col.582, November 3 to November 20 1936–7.
43. House of Commons *Debates*, Fifth Series, vol.317, col.958, November 3 to November 20 1936–7.
44. National Council of Labour, *Minutes and Papers*, report to NCL, 24 November 1936, NMHL.
45. *The Guardian*, 13 November 1936.
46. MEPO: 2/3097, PRO; CAB 24/264 c.p..256, 12 October 1936, PRO.
47. CAB 24/264: c.p. 256, 12 October 1936, PRO.
48. *Ministry of Labour Gazette*, July 1936, p.238
49. House of Commons *Debates*, Fifth Series, vol.317, col.1894 and 1897, November 3 to November 20 1936–7.
50. D. Dougan, *Jarrow March* (Jarrow, 1976), p.92.
51. T10/32 *Borough of Jarrow Council Minutes* 1936–7, 27 April 1937, p.282, TWAS.
52. BT 104/11, *The Manchester Guardian*, 23 November 1938, PRO.
53. CAB 24/264 cp. 229, Memorandum from Sir Kingsley Wood and Ernest Brown on the situation in Merthyr Tydfil. 27 August 1936, PRO.
54. CAB 23/85, 2 September 1936, PRO.
55. CAB 24/265 cp.299, 300, 315, PRO; CAB 23/85, 2 September 1936, PRO; CAB 23/86, 4 November and 17 November 1936, PRO.
56. Compare Communist Party of Great Britain, Wal Hannington papers, National Hunger March press cuttings 1936, NMLH and Ellen Wilkinson papers, WI/07: Newspaper cuttings 1936, NMLH.

George Garrett and the Collective Memory of War

Michael Murphy

Coming to any writer at some distance of time brings obvious difficulties. When that writer is largely unknown, as is the case with George Garrett, these difficulties are exacerbated. Historical periods have a tendency to become associated in our minds with a single figure or, as was the case with Garrett's contemporaries the poets W. H. Auden, Stephen Spender, Cecil Day Lewis and Louis MacNeice—jokingly referred to by the collective name of 'Macspaunday'—with a composite figure that tends to smooth out or ignore those points of difference and divergence that mark out writers of the same generation. This is perhaps a particular danger with the relatively recent past, a past which we may think we know because its events and personalities remain a part of the fabric of our everyday experience. If, then, we are to get the measure of Garrett's work, with its deliberate provocations and the various ways in which it engages with a number of key debates and orthodoxies of 1930s literature and politics, and the ways in which these things come down to us as the fabric of history, then we must attempt to return Garrett to some kind of context. While such important recent studies as Andy Croft's *Red Letter Days: British Fiction in the 1930s* and Valentine Cunningham's *British Writers of the Thirties* mention Garrett by name and reputation, his writings go undiscussed. An exception is provided by Adrian Wright in his 1998 biography of John Lehmann. Wright has clearly read some of Garrett's stories, commenting on their 'Conradian intensity' and ability to 'manage the shift into symbolism with aplomb.'[1] Discussion and appreciation of Garrett's achievement before the outbreak of war in 1939, however, was of a very different order. Not surprisingly, it was leading figures from the left who recognised the importance of his work. One such figure was Sylvia Townsend Warner, who praised Garrett's 'serious outlook upon mankind', about which more later. Another writer who recognised his significance was George Orwell.

In 'The Proletarian Writer' Orwell cites Garrett's 'sea stories' as evidence of the fact that Britain was 'passing into a classless period, and what we call proletarian literature is one of the signs of the change.'[2] Indeed, the fullest contemporary record we have of Garrett appears in 'The Road to Wigan Pier Diary', in which Orwell describes the visit he made Liverpool on 25 February 1936, where he was introduced to Garrett by John Stanley Deiner, a telephone engineer to whom Orwell had been given a letter of introduction by John Middleton Murray. 'I was very greatly impressed by Garrett,' Orwell writes, continuing:

> Had I known before that it is [Garrett] who writes under the pseudonym of Matt Low in the *Adelphi* and one or two other places, I would have taken steps to meet him earlier. He is a biggish hefty chap of about 36, Liverpool-Irish, brought up a Catholic but now a Communist. He says he has had about 9 months work in (I think) the last 6 years. He went to sea as a lad and was at sea about 10 years, then worked as a docker. During the war he was torpedoed on a ship that sank in 7 minutes, but they had expected to be torpedoed and had got their boats ready, and were all saved except the wireless conductor, who refused to leave his post until he had got an answer. He also worked in an illicit brewery in Chicago during Prohibition, saw various hold-ups, saw Battling Siki immediately after he had been shot in a street brawl, etc. etc. all this however interests him much less than Communist politics. I urged him to write his autobiography, but, as usual, living in about two rooms on the dole with a wife (who I gather objects to his writing) and a number of kids, he finds it impossible to settle to any long work and can do only short stories. Apart from the enormous unemployment in Liverpool it is almost impossible for him to get work because he is blacklisted everywhere as a Communist.

It is the differences between Orwell's and Garrett's style of writing, and the influence on it of their social background, that led John Lehmann to draw a comparison between the two. In 'The Man In The Street' from *New Writing In Europe* (1940), Lehmann summarises Orwell's *Road To Wigan Pier* as 'a very fascinating document of the stages of disillusionment through which a middle-class young man can go about the world in which he was brought up.' He then goes on to discuss Garrett:

> It is interesting to compare Orwell's attitude and style with that of a writer, equally vigorous and uncompromising, of actual working-class parentage and upbringing. George Garrett published several stories in *Left Review* and the first series of *New Writing*, and though he has, to many people's regret, not published anything since, he has remarkable powers of unsentimental and lively description, and of pugnacious humour. A seaman from the North of England, he was an old militant in the workers' movement, and

as might be expected is at his best when dealing with events in the day-to-day struggle in which he himself took an active part. He is also concerned to convey all the sordid sights and disgusting smells in the surroundings of people living on the poverty line, but in comparison with Orwell's his descriptions are more robust: the needle of his sensitivity does not quiver so violently as Orwell's, who hates and despises all the things Garrett does but knows them in a far less familiar way.[3]

It appears from this that Lehmann was unaware of the four stories Garrett had had published under the pseudonym of Matt Low (after the French *matelot*, a sailor) in the *Adelphi* between June 1934 and November 1935. Added to the fact that, though Orwell knew 'Matt Low's' stories, there is nothing to suggest that he suspected it to be a pseudonym, this may point to an important reason why later critics have overlooked Garrett's work. Of the eleven stories Garrett published, almost half appear as Matt Low. As far as most readers were concerned George Garrett and Matt Low were two unrelated writers, with the result that the actual scale of Garrett's achievement remained unacknowledged.

This need to translate himself, to create an alter ego, is in itself not without significance. It may owe something to Garrett's notoriety as a political militant (about which more later) or the influence of the Wobblies and others in disguising actual historical figures behind the mask of fictional characterisation, a practice which, as we shall see, Garrett uses to effect in his reportage. But it may also have something to do with the anxieties expressed in a story such as 'The Overcoat' where Bert, whose brother is dying from pneumonia, borrows his brother's overcoat in order to impress a girlfriend. The result is that he is mistaken for his more academic brother—'That fellow has the right stuff in him. What a headpiece! His last lecture was unanswerable'—a mistake he is reluctant to put right.[4] Perhaps, like Bert, Garrett feared being 'discovered', in which case the decision to assume a fictional identity may hint at a certain insecurity about his place as a writer.

Jerry Dawson, a student teacher when he first met Garrett in 1937, touched on precisely such tensions and anxieties.[5] Replying to a query in 1955 from Bruce Bain at *Tribune* as to Garrett's circumstances and whereabouts, Dawson outlined first those social and political conditions that brought Garrett's writing to prominence before suggesting reasons why, post-war, the times were no longer propitious for working-class writers:

> In the late thirties G.G. played a big part in the establishment of Merseyside Unity Theatre (or Left Theatre as it was then called). He had some experience while in America with the Princetown Group, and in

England he had already taken the leading part in a Merseyside production of O'Neill's *The Hairy Ape*. His first parts in Unity were what might have been expected. He played Agate Keller in *Waiting for Lefty* and Driscoll in *Bury the Dead*—and it is unlikely that they were ever played better anywhere, for all George's experience, not only in this country, but even more in the Wobbly movement in the USA. went into them. In these years, too, it was not only G.G.'s ability as an actor that was invaluable to such a theatre group but even more what he was as a man. Many of us learned much more about the meaning of socialism from our contact with him than we did from Left Book Club choices, *Left Review*, or *New Writing*.

Perhaps in the post-war period the day of working-class document, of 'reportage', and all that was over. Certainly the collapse of a number of magazines in which this kind of writing appeared made it difficult to see any strong hopes of publication. But, even if the chances had been greater, it is doubtful if George would have written very much—and for reasons which are so seldom taken into account even by teachers who expect boys from crowded working-class homes to turn out pages of homework. For the writing, like the homework, has to be done on the end of a kitchen table; with the demands of children who need a referee while they emulate Joe Louis and Baksi; with the knowledge that there is much to be done about the house and that 'scribbling' doesn't count as work; even, in the case of corporation tenement houses, with the quarrels of the neighbours reverberating through the thin walls. It can, I suppose, be done—but at least there's enough there to explain why it isn't done more often even by men who have so much to offer as George Garrett has.[6]

The past, Maurice Halbwachs wrote, 'is not preserved but is reconstructed on the basis of the present.'[7] In comparison to Henri Bergson, whose student he was for a while, Halbwachs came to regard our experience of time not as primarily intuitive and subjective but as a social and collective process. '[T]he greatest number of our memories,' he says, 'come back to us when our parents, our friends, or other persons recall them to us. [I]t is in society that people normally acquire their memories. It is also in society that they recall, recognize, and localize their memories.'[8] Halbwachs' ideas are important, and provide us with a theoretical model within which to consider Garrett's writing. It is a model which can suggest ways in which personal experience and memory interact, ways explored by such classics of the 1930s as Orwell's *Homage to Catalonia* (1938) or Isherwood's *Goodbye to Berlin* (1939). And it is in the context of these works and certain aspects of Halbwachs' sociological approach that I want to examine Garrett's stories and reportage as they pertain to a literature of collective memory.

Autobiographical and historical memory

Garrett had brought home to him early the competing claims of belief and ideology as they are determined and defined by those forces scrutinised by Halbwachs. Born on 13 August 1896 in Seacombe, on the opposite bank of the Mersey to Liverpool, his father, Sam, was a confectioner and a member of the Loyal Orange Lodge. His mother, Katherine (née McAllister), came from a family of Irish Republican Catholics. Given the sectarian divisions that still existed in Liverpool at the time, it comes as no surprise that Garrett's parents argued vociferously about his religious upbringing and education. In the end his strong-willed mother won out and he was educated at St Vincent's Catholic school.

Early in Garrett's childhood there seems to have been some comedown in his father's business and the family moved across the water to Liverpool. The evidence is that his father had to take work as a stevedore, loading and unloading ships on the docks. The family rented a house in the Park Lane district of the city which, adjoining Canning Place, formed the centre of what was traditionally known as the seamen's ghetto. The area merged with the equally rundown Scotland Road, haunt of the dockers. Though the family was poor, it was not on the breadline. Many of their neighbours were, however, and Garrett saw schoolchildren attending class without any shoes, sometimes dressed in the ragged hand-me-downs of a deceased grandparent. Once at school the poorest children were often subjected to humiliating comments from teachers and regular assaults by priests. Religious tensions at home, plus incidents such as witnessing one boy in his class being picked on by a bullying priest, clearly made a great impression on Garrett, as the semi-autobiographical 'Apostate' testifies.

It is hardly surprising, therefore, that Garrett's writing consistently questions precisely those sites of cultural authority that concerned Halbwachs: the family, the army, and the hierarchies of social class. At his most straightforward Garrett records and to varying degrees analyses the economic difficulties of young newly weds, the ritual humiliations and petty bullying suffered by schoolchildren, the psychological terrors experienced by those threatened with losing a roof over their heads, the stresses and strains of life 'on the parish', and the harsh discipline of military and naval life. Drawn directly from life, they are the themes and situations we might expect from a writer with Garrett's background. As such, they provide an example of what Halbwachs saw as the important part played by autobiographical memory in reinforcing links with other members of our immediate family, links which are in danger of being broken if they aren't periodically rehearsed.[9] However, Garrett's writing goes further than this narrower form of remembrance and engages with historical memory. This, Halbwachs says, most often reaches us through the written word or other types of semi-public record, like photography. It is a form of memory that is kept alive through such communal activities as official commemorations, festivals, parades etc. It is these influences that help define and instruct us socially, culturally and, of course, politically; and it is on these, as we will see, that Garrett often focuses his attention.

Approached along these lines stories such as 'The Redcap', 'Apostate' and 'Swords Into Ploughshares' can be seen as instructing the reader in tactics for renouncing oppressive authority. Garrett's work can therefore be seen as a part of that tradition of working-class literature which associates a text's authority with its ability to reproduce authentic lived experiences. Where Garrett markedly differs from such texts, though, is his inclusion of events that he did not directly experience. Among the most notable of these, while being perhaps the easiest to overlook, is the Boer War and the subsequent lives of the men who survived it.

The legacy of South Africa

Now all but forgotten because of the two world wars that followed hard on its heels, the Boer War, as Jonathan Lewis has written, can be seen as the precursor of all twentieth century conflicts:

> When people take up a fight against a mighty power and turn it into a guerrilla war, [w]hen soldiers advance under creeping artillery fire, or shoot rapid-firing, high-powered rifles from trenches, [w]hen civilians have their homes looted and burned and are herded into cattle trucks and packed off to the concentration camps, look back to the Boer War.[10]

The evidence is that Garrett and others understood some of these things, especially the need to listen to and learn from the experiences of those men who saw active service in South Africa. In a number of his best stories, particularly 'The Redcap' and 'Swords into Ploughshares', the central characters are veterans of the Boer War who, as Garrett himself did, are now serving on board merchant vessels during the First World War. In both stories it is left to these characters to show their younger comrades how to deal with, and ultimately circumvent, military authority. In 'The Redcap' this responsibility falls to McMahon, whose 'frayed South African war ribbons seemed ridiculously out-of-date to the other men in the forecastle.'[11] In 'Swords into Ploughshares' it is left to Mangor, who has 'soldiered in scattered parts of the Empire', to recognise under the gleaming medals pinned to the ship's captain's chest the more prosaic nature of his heroism:

> The aged skipper was already seated there, gaudily dressed and looking intensely patriotic. On his breast were pinned the South Africa ribbons awarded for transporting horses and corned beef to defeat the Boers.[12]

However, the tactics used by both characters could not be more different. For while McMahon's experience of the hardships, and hard knocks, of war leads him to equate justice with summary execution, Mangor, following the example of a yet older soldier and sailor, attempts to escape military life by feigning madness. Unlike Odysseus, he is successful:

> When the doctor had gone ashore, the skipper wasted no time in completing the arrangements for Mangor's transfer to hospital. Some of the crew good naturedly helped Mangor to dress and linked him down the ship's gangway to the waiting ambulance. They took little notice of his mumbling, 'Now you see how it's done,' nor the queer grin on his face.
> But the Chief saw it and knew the bitterness of defeat.[13]

There are specific historical reasons why, having grown up in Liverpool, George Garrett should later recount the experiences of men who served in South Africa. Of all the British regiments to see action during the campaign it was the 2nd Royal Lancasters who served the longest spell of continuous duty. And there were other regiments involved from the North West of England, namely the Lancashire Fusiliers and two companies of the South Lancashire Regiment. As a significant number of these regiments were made up of men from Liverpool, the impact of the war's most notorious battle, Spion Kop, when the 2nd Royal Lancasters sustained the single greatest loss of life of any unit during the war, was profound. Indeed, so traumatic and long lasting were the events of the battle that in 1906, at the suggestion of a local journalist, a terrace at Liverpool FC's ground was named Spion Kop in honour of the men who fell that day in January 1900.

The battle was witnessed by the special correspondent of the *Manchester Guardian* who, perhaps fearing for his job if he went too far in his condemnation of the British tactics, allowed the final words of his report to be spoken by a Boer doctor. We can assume that the dreadful irony of his words was unintentional:

> A doctor told me of the scene on Spion Kop...A great proportion of the wounds had been made by shells; therefore they must not be described. [He] looked at the dead bodies of men and horses, the litter, the burnt grass where the shells had set fire to it—at the whole sad and splendid scene where the finest infantry in the world had suffered. 'No!' he said, with double truth, 'we Boers would not, could not, suffer like that.'

Spion Kop was a military disaster and remains a monument to a British army riven by class. This much was apparent even to as partial an observer as Winston Churchill, who, as war correspondent for the *Morning Post*, witnessed the ignominious retreat, noting that the battle 'redound[ed] to the honour of the soldiers, though not greatly to that of the generals.' However, even this admission carried a sting in the tail:

> But when all that will be written about this has been written, and all the bitter words have been said by the people who never do anything themselves, the wise and just citizen will remember that these same generals are, after all, brave, capable, noble English gentlemen, trying their best to carry through a task which may prove impossible.[14]

Tragically, the conclusions Churchill drew from the debacle are all too familiar. The distinction he drew between the 'wise and just citizen' (who really must learn not to speak out of turn) and the 'noble English gentlemen' (who, dammit, are doing their level best) is a philosophy of class and power which was to contribute to the deaths of thousands in the trenches of northern Europe. It was also an attitude which, in 1911, led Churchill, then British home secretary, to crack down on the democratic rights of the seamen's union and their supporters to organise themselves in protest against low levels of pay.

The monthly wage of a sailor on an ordinary cargo vessel in 1911 was four pound ten. The seamen wanted ten shillings more, and in the summer of 1911 they went on strike. 'From this,' Harold Hikins writes,

> arose a complicated and tremendous movement which convulsed Merseyside for at least seventy-two days; a movement which was an interwoven complex of several strikes involving at one time or another every section of transport workers in the port and culminating in a general strike of all sections; a movement which was at the same time part of a national, and even international, upheaval of mounting proportions, only cut short by world war. The Liverpool strikes were also part of the national seamen's strike of June and of the national railway strike of August; and separate local strikes of carters, tramwaymen, dockers, tugmen, bargemen, coal-heavers and others broke out in many parts of Britain throughout the period. We must bear this in mind, while we are concentrating on Liverpool events: Liverpool was spearheading a national movement.[15]

The mood of the protest was generally peaceful. The strikers knew the police, the police knew the strikers. Neither side had anything to gain from violence. Despite this Churchill likened the situation to a civil war. When the city magistrates appealed to him for assistance, he ordered, on Wednesday 9 August, that police from Leeds and Birmingham travel to Liverpool's Lime Street station. Throughout the rest of the week the build-up of forces continued. Police arrived from Lancashire and Bradford, while contingents of the Royal Warwickshire, Scots Greys, Hussars, and Yorkshire Regiments were stationed in and around the city centre. By the weekend there were an estimated 5,000 troops and 2,400 police at the disposal of the head constable. 'If troops not sufficient', Churchill wired the lord mayor, 'you should ask for more.'[16] While Churchill denied to Parliament that the government was siding with the employers, it was apparent that the build-up of police and troops was meant to coincide with the demonstration planned by the strike committee to take place at St. George's Plateau.

On Sunday 13 August, later known as 'Red' or 'Bloody' Sunday, an estimated 60,000 people turned up in sweltering heat to show their support for the strikers. Among them was George Garrett, whose fifteenth birthday it was. Herded into the square, the strikers and their supporters listened to Tom Mann, chairman of the strike committee, defying Churchill to do his utmost: 'Let him send ten times as many military to Liverpool. Let him parade every street with them. Let him send his gunboats up the Mersey. But all the King's Forces and all the King's men won't take the vessels out of the docks to sea again.'[17]

As the speech continued there was a small disturbance in nearby Lord Nelson Street. The authorities panicked and told the police to clear the area.[18] Mann was replaced at the podium by a magistrate who read the Riot Act while mounted police charged in using long truncheons. Garrett himself was struck full in the face by a baton, sustaining a broken nose and several smashed teeth.

In the days that followed the 'Liverpool Peterloo', there were running street battles between the strikers and police. In some areas of the city it became unsafe for a policeman to walk alone. Another consequence of the troubles was that Protestants and Catholics who had long waged constant guerrilla warfare now took the opportunity openly to settle old scores. We can only imagine the effect this must have had on Garrett's parents, but the following year, as a result of 'family tension', Garrett left home and began sleeping out, 'mostly in an old stables near the docks'.[19] He decided to leave the city and stowaway on board a ship bound for Buenos Aires.

By the time Garrett began writing his sea stories in the 1930s he hadn't been to sea for almost a decade. To write about the sea was, therefore, always to write about the past. Yet there is no sense that the intervening years tempered either his passion for life below decks nor his anger at the injustices he witnessed there. But unlike his autobiographical treatment of childhood in 'Apostate', where his experience of poverty and religious intolerance and violence in Liverpool are frankly dealt with, his sea stories only ever hint at the European-wide violence and terrors of the Great War. Rather, it is the effect war had on dehumanising man's relationship with man that Garrett focuses on. As in James Hanley's *Hollow Sea*, the war in Garrett's stories takes place largely off-stage. For the men on board a merchant ship there were always more urgent problems.

The 1922 Hunger March

In the immediate aftermath of the First World War the nature and even the desirability of heroism was widely questioned. 'This book,' wrote Wilfrid Owen in the 'Preface' to his *Collected Poems*, 'is not about heroes'. And in *Memoirs of A Fox-Hunting Man*, Siegfried Sassoon felt confident that although heroic thoughts might do for officers, they no longer suited the common soldiery. By the 1930s, however, this post-war refusal to engage in heroics was being challenged by political events at home and on the continent. And though Garrett never dealt explicitly with the crisis, this is not to say that there aren't a number of stories that deal with it *implicitly*.

Garrett's militancy, or what others termed militancy, was commented on by many who knew him. He certainly favoured direct action over talk, and must therefore have felt some anxiety during the 1930s about his role as a writer. These tensions might be seen as surfacing in 'Letter Unsigned' where an unnamed seaman, trapped within the forecastle, scribbles a last letter while the tramp steamer he is on board sinks. Writing to keep up his spirits, and remembering having once seen wine-casks floating 'when the tops were almost flush with the water', he questions whether the hopelessness of the situation means that he should behave like the other men in the room: 'And because they are too paralysed to move, does that say I must sit moping, too?'[20] As the water climbs higher and his companions give way to despair, the narrator clings to the last vestiges of his humanity: memory and language.

Too old himself to fight, Garrett's writings find him sympathising with neither his own generation nor the generation about to fight a second world war, but those men he knew and worked alongside who had seen action in South Africa. There are a number of reasons why he would have done this. One, as we have seen, is to do with the connections between the Battle of Spion Kop and Liverpool. The other is that Garrett was interested in showing how wartime experiences and patterns of behaviour can became a part of civilian life.

A clear example of this is 'Liverpool 1921–1922', in which Garrett shows how Liverpool's unemployed organised themselves in opposition to the city authorities:

> Ex-officers (a few) and NCOs (hundreds), were ticked off for easy reference. All were re-grouped under district headings, then sub-divided into neighbourhood units of twelve under the control of an ex-NCO who now ranked as street captain. The men by knowing each other could check up on strangers. They had in mind the possibility of plain-clothes detectives joining the organisation for disruptive purposes. A double check against this was the grudge the unemployed police-strikers bore towards those who had taken their jobs.
>
> A list of duties was agreed upon. Street captains were to be responsible for unit discipline and conduct. From amongst themselves they would elect a leader for their own district. All district leaders would be answerable to the disciplinary section of the second committee.
>
> The most dominant figure of this committee was the ex-sergeant major. Still under forty years of age, he had been an all-round athlete, heavy-weight boxer, and physical instructor. The privations of two years unemployment had left him almost a wreck. His face was white and drawn. His clothes were baggy and threadbare.[21]

Garrett's record of these years and the actions taken by the hungry men and women is a remarkable document. In 1921 unemployment in Liverpool had reached 60,000. Workhouses turned the starving away from the door and demobbed soldiers, home from the killing fields of Flanders and the Somme, were forced to pawn their hard-won medals. It includes not only a description of the hardships suffered by the unemployed and their families but a vivid portrait of how the city's authorities ruthlessly crushed any organised protest.

The piece ends with a description of how the National Unemployed Workers' Movement, given the refusal of either the politicians or trades unions to practically support the principle of 'Work or Maintenance', took the decision to organise a protest march to London. The aim was to convince the country at large that 'a national tragedy [be] treated as a national problem'.

The march coincided with a hastily called general election, the Tories having reneged on the coalition government led by Lloyd George. Throughout the two weeks of electioneering the marchers—including iron-and-steel workers from Scotland, shipyard workers of the Tyne, shipwrights of Barrow-in-Furness, dockers and seamen from Liverpool, miners from Cumberland and South Wales, cotton workers from Lancashire, and engineers from the Midlands—carried their banners from town to town. They arrived in London on 17 November, two days after the election of a Conservative government led by Bonar Law, a British signatory to the Treaty of Versailles, who had campaigned for national solidarity after the rigours and social upheavals of the immediate post-war years. His promise that the nation's most pressing need was 'to get on with its work' clearly didn't apply to the country's industrial heartlands, and Law refused even to meet the marchers' representatives.[22]

First published in *New Writing* in spring 1937, Garrett's eye-witness account of the Liverpool contingent of the 1922 Hunger March, 'The First Hunger March', was subsequently singled out for praise by Sylvia Townsend Warner:

> Garrett's *First Hunger March* [is] an account of men in earnest and a practical joke. The narrative, dry, detailed, and with that art-concealing artfulness which one sees on the serious blank faces of proletarian humorists, joins on without a hitch to the narrative style of Defoe (another tract writer). And whether Garrett is conscious of Defoe…does not appear to be of much importance. The one and the other are exponents of that admirable tradition of a straightforward story with good sense and good feeling behind it—an underlying morality, in fact, a serious outlook upon mankind.[23]

On the surface 'The First Hunger March' would appear to be a simple piece of reportage. To an extent, it is. But it also importantly analyses the underlying economic and political causes of, and connections between, war abroad and crippling unemployment at home. In doing so it gives an identity to those servicemen who, in a poem written at the time of the Hunger March, were described by Ivor Gurney thus:

> Where are they now on State-doles, or showing shop patterns
> Or walking town to town sore in borrowed tatters
> Or begged. Some civic routine one never learns.
> The heart burns—but has to keep out of face how heart burns.[24]

Garrett, however, was never shy of showing exactly how and why 'heart burns'. Neither was he afraid of demonstrating in his writings the connection between outbreaks of violence due to economic disenfranchisement and conflicts involving nation states.

The anonymous narrator of 'The First Hunger March' begins his account with the information that

> The men responsible for the initial organisation of the march, having

learned much from capitalist warfare, vested leadership in those who as non-commissioned officers had handled men in the army....All recognised the need for discipline in their determination to reach London. From field, factory, mine, and dockyard they had gathered; a miniature army with a purpose, not a rabble cadging for bread.[25]

While the description of ex-servicemen marching on London is of course reminiscent of the so-called Peasant's Revolt of 1381, led by the ex-soldier Wat Tyler, the conditions which the men meet on their journey to London are reminiscent of a more recent conflict.

Arriving at one town (to protect the guilty Garrett allows it to go unnamed) the marchers are horrified to discover conditions at the local workhouse:

Local families whose home life had been broken up on entering the workhouse were now compelled as inmates to live separate existences. A high-wire netting divided the workhouse grounds into sections. Through this, wives conversed with husbands, and children with their fathers. Some of the marchers stared in amazement as little tots pressed their lips to the wire in awkward kisses for their fathers, stooped low on the opposite side of the netting.[26]

The marchers' shock and anger is understandable. But we also need to read it in the context of the fact that for some of them such an encounter would have brought back memories of the British policy during the Boer War of putting civilian populations—mostly women and children—into concentration camps. It is therefore an image of wartime experience returning to haunt civilian life, and reminds us of Halbwachs' analysis of one specific location of collective memory and behaviour.

'Despite intervals of peace,' Halbwachs wrote in the *Social Frameworks of Memory*,

there is what may be called a natural and historical species of soldier. That is, there are certain common traits characterizing soldiers in all historical periods that can be explained in terms of the soldier's life in the trenches and camps which only incidentally derives from military tradition.[27]

Here then, in Garrett's description of a 1920s workhouse, is an example of precisely these memories of a 'soldier's life in the trenches and camps'. And though the history of the use of concentration camps in the Boer conflict is too large a subject to adequately do justice to here, several points are worth noting because of the particular angle of light they throw on Garrett's narrative with its deliberate and provocative remembrance of that war.

Looked at from the perspective of Walter Benjamin's 'Angelus Novus', which sees history not as a chain of distinct events but as a 'single catastrophe which keeps piling wreckage upon wreckage',[28] we might recognise the camps which the British established in South Africa as modifications of those compounds covered with wire netting built by De Beers Consolidated Mines under Cecil Rhodes to house the large numbers of black migrant workers needed to mine the enormous concentration of diamonds around Kimberley. This may seem to be pushing an analogy too far, but the two are directly linked. For though Rhodes controlled the mines, the question of who owned the land surrounding them was more contentious and was a direct cause of the conflagration which, between 1899 and 1902, consumed some 22,000 British and colonial troops, 7,000 Boers, upwards of 20,000 Black Africans, and 28,000 non-combatants—the vast majority of them children—who died in the British-run camps.

A literature of collective memory

Perhaps this is a suitable point at which to ask whether Garrett's stories are pessimistic or optimistic about the future of the working class. His own experience taught him that the struggle for equality of education, housing, employment and legal representation was one fraught with disappointments, and it would have been easy for him to become cynical. There is no evidence that he did so. Sceptical, yes. A great deal of the humour of Garrett's writing emerges from the point where scepticism becomes allied with satire. It is an attitude, as with so much that we find in his writing, that is drawn directly from life.

'The First Hunger March' concludes with the mock burial of a tin of bully beef. Part mummer's play, part agit-prop, the scene provides us with a self-portrait of Garrett with his 'blubbery priest's face'. More importantly it offers a scathing attack on a British establishment that failed to provide working class men and women with an opportunity to work. And it is this section of the population that Garrett saw as making up his readership. For throughout the piece it is assumed that the reader is on the side of the marchers, and when one of them—the unnamed Garrett with his blubbery face—adopts the guise of a priest in order the deceive the town's population we are let in early on the joke:

> Very quickly the 'priest' was dressed: collar back to front; a piece of black sleeve-lining down his chest, and a silk hat on his head. The coachman next brought out a mournful-looking overcoat, buttoned it on the 'priest', then stood away a few paces. While flicking off some pieces of chaff he burst out laughing.

'You look the real McCoy, now,' he said. 'By Jeese you do.'[29]

But if the Church comes in for a bit of gentle ridicule, the men's real scorn is reserved for the military. Again it is the disguised Garrett who applies the coup de grâce:

> 'Friends,' he began with an ecclesiastical drawl. 'We are gathered here to pay a last tribute to our dearly departed comrade, B.B. The greatness of our empire is in no mean measure due to him. He served on all fronts in the last war. A very old soldier, he saw service in the Boer War. He was always at hand, and could be rushed anywhere in an emergency. We are mindful of the praise lavished on prominent generals; and begrudge not the fame of two other names, none of us are likely to forget, Tickler and Maconachie;[30] but with all due respect to them, our late comrade B.B. was the real backbone of the British army. The song says, 'Old soldiers never die,' but like everything else they must die eventually. And comrade B.B. has ended his days with us. May he rest in peace.'[31]

We might wonder if Garrett isn't here commenting not only on the passing of an old soldier but on the British Empire itself. Certainly the mock funeral takes the trappings of Imperial power—flags, firing squads, military and religious costume, kettle drums, disciplined marching, the Bible—and circumvents their authority by using them to expose the ideology of power. In other words a fiction is used to undermine another fiction. Hardly surprising if the crowds gathered to watch the spectacle 'stared and blinked' when the Union Jack was thrown back to reveal the 'tin of bully beef...set in the middle, and the wreath hung on top like a crowning laurel.' In form and content, therefore, 'The First Hunger March' allies itself with a range of radical political causes. Obviously it supports the aims of the men who marched on London in the early 1920s; but going beyond this it advocates the continuing use of art as a means of bringing about a just society.

The memory of working on board ships and the later day-to-day actuality of the struggle to find dockside work: out of these disparate experiences and influences George Garrett wrote stories and reportage of personal witness which, in turn, became part of a literature of collective memory. We have seen how 'The First Hunger March' can be read in exactly this way, with Garrett's account revealing the connections between the events of 1922 and those of the 1914–1918 war and, before that, the Boer War. When it was first published in 1937 the account must also have reminded his contemporaries of the hunger marches of the early 1930s, most recently the National Hunger March of 1936 and the same year's 'Jarrow Crusade'. Garrett's literature of collective memory can thus be seen as being a part of the tradition of didactic working-class literature, a tradition which famously includes Tressell's *The Ragged Trousered Philanthropist,* and which challenges orthodox histories. The purpose of the writer, as Garrett wrote in his essay 'Conrad's "Nigger of the *Narcissus*"', is 'to portray life whole' while recognising the personal limitations of such an ideal:

> [I]t is almost impossible for an artist or anyone else to see life whole. Seeing is determined by an awareness of intense experience, but does not always exclude personal prejudices. And personal prejudices must not pass as whole truth.[32]

In looking to realise this vision in his art Garrett was an advocate—a militant advocate—of tolerance. As such, his life and his writing are of a piece. It seems fitting, therefore, that his last public appearances were as a speaker during the seaman's strike of spring 1966. He died of throat cancer on 28 May that same year.

Notes

1. Adrian Wright, *John Lehmann. A pagan adventure* (London, 1998), p.94.
2. Sonia Orwell and Ian Angus (eds), *The Collected Essays, Journalism and Letters of George Orwell. Volume 1. An age like this 1920–1940* (London, 1968), p.42.
3. John Lehmann, *New Writing in Europe* (London, 1940), pp.83–4.
4. George Garrett, *The Collected George Garrett* (Nottingham, 1999), p.55.
5. Jerry Dawson was later to edit a not always textually reliable collection of Garrett's stories, *Out of Liverpool* (Liverpool, 1982), as well as Garrett's *Liverpool 1921–1922* (Liverpool, 1982).
6. The National Museums and Libraries hold this letter and other material relevant to Garrett and Liverpool's Unity Theatre as part of the Merseyside Unity Theatre Archive.
7. Maurice Halbwachs, *On Collective Memory* (Chicago, 1992), p.40.
8. Halbwachs, *Memory*, p.38.
9. Halbwachs, *Memory*, p.24.
10. Tabitha Jackson, *The Boer War* (London, 1999), pp.6–7.
11. Garrett, *Garrett*, p.79.
12. Garrett, *Garrett*, p.164.
13. Garrett, *Garrett*, p.169.
14. Winston S. Churchill, *Frontiers and Wars* (New York, 1995), p.437.
15. Harold Hikins, *Strike. The Liverpool General Transport Strike 1911* (Merseyside, 1980), p.1.
16. Hikins, *Strike*, pp.18–20.
17. Quoted from Alan O'Toole's unpublished typescript, *George Garrett: Seaman, Syndicalist and Writer*, Raymond Williams Centre, Nottingham Trent University.
18. Hikins, *Strike*, p.22.
19. O'Toole, *George Garrett: Seaman*.

20. Garrett, *Garrett*, p.92.
21. Garrett, *Garrett*, p.209.
22. Arriving in London, Garrett was one of the marchers who addressed the gathered crowds. 'We do not want,' he said in typically bullish fashion, 'to go back to our towns and tell the people that the comrades in London gave us a clap, that they treated us very fine. We want to say that our comrades in London are preparing not for the tranquillity that suits Mr Bonar Law, but the tranquillity that will suit the working class.' See Peter Kingsford, *The Hunger Marchers in Britain 1920–1940* (London, 1982), p.49.
23. Sylvia Townsend Warner, 'Underlying Morality' in *Left Review*, July 1937, p.367.
24. Ivor Gurney, in George Walter (ed.), *Rewards of Wonder. Poems of Cotswold, France, London* (Manchester, 2000), p.82.
25. Garrett, *Garrett*, p.224.
26. Garrett, *Garrett*, p.231.
27. Halbwachs, *Memory*, p.161.
28. Walter Benjamin, 'Theses on the Philosophy of History' in *Illuminations* (London, 1992 edn, transl. Harry Zohn), p.249. Although not published until 1950, Benjamin's essay was completed in 1940, a matter of months before his death at the Franco-Spanish border.
29. Garrett, *Garrett*, p.237.
30. A 'tickler' is a rolled cigarette, or the tobacco used for making a cigarette. 'Maconachie' was a kind of tinned meat-and-vegetable stew issued to soldiers in the First World War.
31. Garrett, *Garrett*, p.238.
32. Garrett, *Garrett*, p.240.

Women and Fascism
A critique

David Renton

Elsewhere I have criticised the development of fascism studies, a way of looking at the history of fascism which focuses on the ideas of the far right, to the exclusion of fascist practice.[1] In this article I would like to criticise one strand of fascism studies, namely the recent study of the relationship between gender and fascism. The authors I have in mind are mostly writing in Britain, and several chose British fascism for the object of their historical study. I do not suggest that merely writing about women and British fascism should be problematic. The study becomes controversial when the authors have accepted fascist claims that their movement represented women's interests. Among such authors may be counted Stephen Cullen, Julie Gottlieb and Martin Durham.[2]

The pressure to come up with new theories and new approaches to the subject is intense. Yet the impact of new theories is not always positive. The love of controversy has given a spur towards new approaches, some of which assert the originality of their argument at the expense of the material which would be needed to defend their case. One of the best examples of such provocative theory is Durham's recent book, *Women and Fascism*, which addresses the nature of women's support for fascism and nazism. As its author points out, many millions of women voted for the fascist parties or supported the fascist regimes. Indeed, women often represented Mussolini or Hitler's greatest admirers. The purpose of *Women and Fascism* is summed up in the introduction:

> Conventional accounts see fascism as, by definition, an anti-feminist movement devoted to the removal of women from the labour market and their return to a life of domestic servitude and the unceasing production of children...In important ways, this study is intended to subvert that supposition.[3]

Durham establishes that fascism was a feminist issue, but he has more difficulty in making the case that fascism was itself a feminist movement. His difficulties might be compared to those of a comparable historian of Islamic fundamentalism. It is agreed that many Islamist parties have received their strongest support from women, but how far does that make these organisations objectively *women's* parties? The most persuasive test would lie in the practice of the ideology, not only in the character of its membership, but more in the extent to which women are involved in the actual running of the organisation, in the ideas which are promulgated, and in the nature of the laws which are introduced if and when the movement achieves state power.[4]

An anti-feminist ideology

Tested in these ways, Durham's own research makes it clear that fascism was an unmistakably anti-feminist ideology. In Italy, Mussolini campaigned to return women into the family, insisting that Italian birth-rates were too low. Contraception was banned and feminism described as a 'Jewish' invention. Within Hitler's party, women made up just six to eight per cent of the membership. The British Union of Fascists (BUF) may have been more sympathetic to women than its sister parties, and a minority of its writers did accept that women might have a right to work. Yet even in this, Durham's home case, the party as a whole was eugenicist, fixated with increased birth-rates, and opposed to women's independence. Indeed the third chapter of *Women and Fascism* demonstrates that the few recognisable feminists within fascism (including Mary Richardson and Mrs Carrington) left the BUF precisely because it would not meet their demands.[5]

All these examples are taken from Durham's book, although it would be possible to add further evidence of fascism's hostility to women's independence which has been discovered by other historians over the past twenty years. The favourite starting point for many traditional histories of gender and fascism has been Weimar Germany. According to Anne Alexander, this was a relatively liberal and female-friendly society, a positive example of women's relative equality:

> Women gained the vote in 1918, and by 1919, ten per cent of the delegates elected to the National Assembly were female. Between 1919 and 1932, 112 women were elected as deputies to serve in the Reichstag. Many women activists had high hopes that this signalled a permanent change in German politics. Maria Juchacz, a Socialist argued: 'The Woman Question in Germany no longer exists in the old sense of the term. It has been solved.'
>
> Liberation meant more than the chance to vote. Weimar Germany witnessed a cultural flowering which seemed to promise both sexual and artistic fulfilment…More than 150,000 Germans subscribed to the jour-

nals of sex reformers such as Magnus Hirschfeld and Helene Stöcker, the leading figure in the radical *Bund für Mutterschutz*. Music hall songs celebrated women's sexual and political confidence: 'Chuck all the men out of the Reichstag' was one popular chorus.[6]

Yet in power, the NSDAP attempted to ban women from professional work. It introduced marriage loans, dependent both on the political loyalty of the family, and on the woman's consent to give up paid employment. Nazi racism also had a particular impact on women. It was mothers who would breed the new race of fit Germans, free from racial and political taint. The implementation of eugenic policy meant an unprecedented increase in the state supervision of the birth process. Older women were surplus to requirements. Younger women could only hope that their child would not be one of the 100,000 Germans killed in cold blood for disability, lost limbs, inherited social weaknesses and the like. The contrast between Weimar and what was to follow could not be more striking.

Richard Evans has described how after Hitler's victory in 1933, even Nazi women's organisations felt a need to condemn the independent status of women. So Gertrud Bäumer, the leading figure in the BDF supported women who resigned from political office in the early 1930s and retreated into the home, on the grounds that the rough and tumble of politics was 'foreign to women's natures'.[7] In a similar vein, Claudia Koonz has carefully documented the experience of women in the regime's descent into murder. The Nazi eugenics program treated women's bodies as factories for the production of children. Unfit mothers were sterilised, and others were killed in the Holocaust.[8] Similar observations have been made for the unequal status of women in Mussolini's Italy.[9]

Thus there is a considerable body of work which is rejected because its analysis of women's roles lacks 'complexity', and because any crude account of women's lives will write real people out of history. In *Women and Fascism,* Durham skates over the contradictions between argument and evidence by invoking a series of yes-buts. 'Italian Fascism was not ascribed with anti-feminism from its beginnings…The party was not uniformly misogynist…A closer examination suggests a more complex picture…Nazism is not to be understood as the uncomplicated expression of patriarchal power…There is more fluidity than we might have thought in fascist notions of the feminine.'[10] According to *Women and Fascism*, women's active involvement in the NF in Britain in the 1970s is demonstrated by the sympathetic treatment that women received in the fascist paper, *Bulldog*.

Which took to publishing regular music reports, accompanied by photos of young women, usually on NF marches. They were sometimes unidentified, sometimes named as members. Thus on one occasion a London member ('The Blonde Bombshell of Southwark') was shown wearing a White Power T-shirt standing in front of a Union Jack. One of the final issues of the publication called for girls who fancied 'being a Bulldog Bird' to 'send a photo of yourself with personal details. The sexier the better…'[11]

Such 'feminism' can hardly be compared to Women's Liberation or the Ruskin Conference.

1970s activism

There are other ways to write about fascism and its impact on women. Twenty-five years ago, the majority assumptions among historians were shaped by the strength of socialist and feminist history, organised in Britain in the History Workshop and other socialist history networks.[12] Members of this milieu did write about fascism, but in a more critical way. One reason for the greater hostility to fascism expressed in their work is that many writers were actively involved in the large anti-racist campaign that was so important in Britain at the end of the 1970s.[13] This campaign gave birth to an array of organisations, including Rock Against Racism, the Anti-Nazi League, Rock Against Sexism and Women Against Racism and Fascism. The contention of this paper is that the activist history produced by writers sympathetic to anti-racism offers a more compelling explanation of the relationship between women and fascism than that offered for example in Durham's recent book. So what did these historians argue?

One important collective was the 'Women and Fascism Study Group', based at the Centre for Contemporary Cultural Studies in Birmingham. This group contributed to a Women Against Racism and Fascism (WARF) conference held in Birmingham in early 1978, and then published a pamphlet of their own, the following year.[14] Their argument was that fascism should not be seen primarily as a racist movement, but rather as a party which was sexist and homophobic as well. In their words, 'Fascism does address women *as women*—or rather, as wives and mothers, breeders for race and nation—and it aims to win support on that basis. Fascism also addresses men—it sees itself as virility personified, and regards liberalism as "feminine".'[15] Members of the group saw the phrase 'breeders for race and nation' as central to their argument, and this became the title of their pamphlet. Having criticised mainstream writers for neglecting the distorted masculine politics at the heart of fascism, the Women and Fascism Study Group did not replace the existing one-sided theories with a further one-sided approach of their own. Instead they sought to integrate their analysis of fascism and sexism into a total argument which also emphasised the racist and nationalistic character of fascism as well. Sections of their pamphlet addressed racism, eugenics, and also the impact of the demand for women's liberation.

One further aspect of the Women and Fascism Study Group pamphlet is worthy of mention. In order to sustain a consistently anti-sexist understanding of fascism in inter-war Italy and Germany and post-war Britain, the authors drew on an earlier generation of witnesses to fascism, including Wilhelm Reich, Virginia Woolf, Winifred Holtby and Maria Macciocchi.[16] I will mention only one of these earlier writers here. Virginia Woolf's 1938 essay 'Three Guineas', asked how to prevent the collapse into fascism and European war. Her conclusion described the fascist invocation of a cult of muscularity:

> Another picture has imposed itself upon the foreground. It is the figure of a man; some say, others deny that he is Man himself, the quintessence of virility, the perfect type of which all the others are imperfect adumbrations. He is a man certainly. His eyes are glazed; his eyes glare. His body, which is braced in an unnatural position, is tightly cased in a uniform. Upon the breast of that uniform are sewn medals and other mystical symbols. His hand is upon a sword. He is called in German and Italian Führer or Duce; in our language Tyrant or Dictator. And behind him lie ruined houses and dead bodies men, women and children.

The importance of this symbol to Woolf was that it raised clearly the connection between 'the public and the private worlds'. A public dictatorship could only become a private dictatorship, a society in which women would be dependent and at home. Yet if fascism made a claim to understand the universal status of Man, so did anti-fascism. 'The human figure even in a photograph suggests other and more complex emotions. It suggests that we cannot disassociate ourselves from that figure but are ourselves that figure.' This discussion provided Woolf's conclusion, the need to challenge the fascist image of universal man: 'we can prevent war not by repeating your worlds and following your methods but by finding new worlds and creating new methods.' It was a message endorsed by the authors of *Breeders for Race and Nation*.[17]

Another group which attempted to study the gender dynamics of fascism was the Liverpool-based socialist group, Big Flame, in a pamphlet, *Sexuality and Fascism*. This was typical of the 1970s' literature, in that it began by stressing the sexist character of fascism, 'Discussions of the ideology of National Socialism has often underestimated, or ignored, the vast importance of their anti-feminist ideas.' What made fascism sexist? First, fascism's anti-liberalism demanded an assault on women's organisation. Second, fascism's racism required control of the birth process, which justified a draconian supervision of the private sphere. Third, fascism's alliance with conservatism reinvigorated the traditional Christian dominance over women's lives. One point at which Big Flame's argument superseded Durham's more recent work was in its treatment of the British fascist organisation, the National Front (NF). Like Durham, Big Flame observed that the NF did recruit a number of women to its organisation. Yet this fact was connected to the contemporary crisis in the family, the rise in divorce and abortion, the emergence of alternative lifestyles and gay sexuality. One of the Front's appeals to women was precisely that it claimed to defend the family. This call may have represented a defence of the subordination of women, but in so far as NF propaganda succeeded, this was not the first time in history that people have supported a demand which was opposed to their own objective interests.[18]

Still in 1970s Britain, the socialist writer Jane Hardy wrote an important article for the magazine *Women's Voice* on 'Women and Fascism'. Her piece argued for anti-fascism from an explicitly socialist feminist perspective. First of all, she described how Hitler's Germany had forced women back into the home. Next she gave examples of how fascist speakers, Hitler and Goebbels had defended their vision of women's role in society. Then Hardy showed that these right-wing ideas had come back to haunt in more recent times:

> What is so sickening is that it is not so very different from what we hear every day; women should give up their jobs, the 1967 Abortion Act should be tightened or restricted or abolished; *Gay News* is threatening our moral fibre. These are not attacks by fascists, but it is a thin line that divides conservative ideas from those of the extreme right.[19]

Women's Voice operated around this time as the main publishing vehicle for another woman's anti-fascist organisation, Women Against the Nazis. For the editors of this magazine, the question of women's relationship to fascism was a consistent theme. In February 1978, *Women's Voice* ran an interview with Miriam Karlin. She was a prominent member of the ANL, responsible for recruiting fellow-actresses, including Mia Farrow, Janet Suzman, Peggy Ashcroft, Glenda Jackson and Dorothy Tutin. Karlin felt that too many men were thinking about their career: 'Women are far more prepared to stand up and be counted on their gut reaction to something.'[20]

Another organisation to mention was Rock Against Sexism, again part of this anti-racist and anti-sexist milieu. In an article for the magazine *Temporary Hoarding* on Wilhelm Reich, a radical psychologist and anti-fascist from Weimar Germany, Lucy Toothpaste, the founder of Rock Against Sexism, attempted to demonstrate that fascism, and indeed all forms of political authoritarianism, represented an onslaught against sex, not just in the 1930s, but forty years later as well:

> In case all that lot seems a bit far-fetched to you, we couldn't resist giving you some living proof of the connection between authoritarianism in the home and in the state. 'Love and discipline went together. My father sometimes took his pit belt off and leathered me. I shed tears, but I knew he was right and I was wrong.' That's what James Anderton said in an interview in the Observer in February. It was a belief that right and wrong were as distinct as black and white that reinforced his one and only ambition 'to be a policeman and if possible the biggest policeman of all.'[21]

Sadly, by 1979 Anderton's goal had been achieved, as Lucy Toothpaste went on to record: 'Well, he grew up to be a policeman alright, the chief constable of Greater Manchester to be exact, the second most powerful cop in the country.'

Mass psychology

The interest in Wilhelm Reich was common across most of the writers in this milieu, but why did he exert such influence? Half of the answer lies outside the question of the relationship between fascism and gender. A Dialectics of Liberation conference was held in 1968 at the London School of Economics. The speakers included R.D. Laing, David Cooper, Lucien Goldmann and Paul Sweezy. The glue binding together this disparate range of economists, psychologists and cultural studies writers was (as one participant David Widgery observes) 'neither Sartre nor Fanon, but the Marxist Reich of the inter-war years'.[22] Taking place at such a pivotal time and location for the counter-culture, this conference had a symbolic appeal and remained a point of reference for the British left for at least the next ten years to come. The other reason for Wilhelm Reich's appeal has more to do with the subject under discussion. Reich's theories appealed to anti-fascist writers in the late 1970s because of his interest in questions of gender, sexuality and the fascist mass movement. So Reich was a key reference point for the authors of *Breeders for Race and Nation*. For them, the significance of Reich lay in his interest in the mass psychology of fascism: 'Reich was one of the few in the 30s to pose the question of why fascism appeals to the mass of men and women. Why did so many join the Nazi movement? What anxieties and fears was fascism addressing? These questions are still central to a feminist and socialist analysis of right wing and fascist movements.'[23]

In order to explain the appeal of fascism, Wilhelm Reich's *The Mass Psychology of Fascism* (1933), combined insights from Marxist economics and

Freudian psychology. For Reich, the crisis of the 1930s was a crisis of sexuality. Capitalism was in crisis, and disrupting the traditional structures of family and sexual life. As a consequence, sexual desires were repressed, both for men and women. Yet fascism appeared to celebrate the sexual unfreedom of women in particular. Political reaction consciously exploited 'the sexual effect of a uniform, the erotically provocative effect of the rhythmically executed goose-stepping'. The classic example of this process was the swastika. Reich believed that this symbol had been chosen for its historic, sexual connotations.[24] Not only did fascism exploit sexuality; it did so in a way understood by its audience: 'The exhibitionistic nature of militaristic procedures have been more practically comprehended by a sales girl or an average secretary than by our most erudite politicians.' The rise of fascism, the adversary of sexual freedom, represented a failure of human creativity, an extended suppressed form of human sexuality, based on an authoritarian machine-civilisation and its 'mechanistic-mythical conception of life.'[25]

These Reichian insights have not been restricted to feminists and others of the left. Since the 1970s, several working historians have attempted to integrate them into more conventional histories of fascism. One such is George Mosse, whose account of fascist sexuality in Hitler's Germany makes much of the relative invisibility of women's bodies in fascist art, compared to the abundance of men's bodies, especially in fascist sculpture. As Mosse documents, even female fascists observed the contradiction implied in the Nazi Party's rhetorical support for procreation when this was combined with an ideological hostility to sex. One such was Lydia Gottschewski, the organiser of the League of German Girls (BDM). Although Gottschewski was an extreme anti-feminist, even she observed that the Nazi denial of bodily love could only reduce the status of German women.[26] Similar perspectives inform Klaus Theweleit's two-volume *Male Fantasies*, a compelling reading of the books and letters produced first by members of the Freikorps, and then by male Nazis. His interest, like Reich's, is in the overlap between fascism as a form of class-rule and fascism as a form of gender-domination. In his words, 'along with capitalist relations of production, a specific male-female (patriarchal) relation might belong at the centre of our examination of fascism, as a producer of life-destroying realities.'[27]

This analysis of fascism has also spread beyond the confines of academic history. The Canadian author Margaret Attwood's novel, *The Handmaid's Tale*, represents an attempt to translate this understanding of fascism into the sphere of literature.[28] In her book, a contemporary clerico-fascism conquers North America, leaving Japanese tourists in their knee-length skirts to photograph the surviving and fully-veiled women, divided into a complex hierarchy of wives, cooks, and biological mothers. Older women disappear, to work in conditions of extreme manual labour in the republic's colonies. The novel's heroine Offred is a handmaid, which means that she is trained to produce the children of her commander. Outside the bedroom, her day is spent wandering veiled head-to-toe, bored and desperate for amusement. Women are also denied the freedom to read and write. Of course, *The Handmaid's Tale* is not a historically accurate account of what fascism was like. The truths of literature are different. Instead the book points in an exaggerated way to one real aspect of historic fascism—namely its intense restriction of the lives of women.

A contradictory movement

From the literature which has been described here, four key points emerge. First, in power fascism represented an attack on women. Considerable attempts were made to remove women from the public sphere of work and politics, and to place women instead in the private sphere of home life. Second, such misogyny was connected to other themes in fascist ideology. For example, fascism's concern with race was part of a general concern with the help of the 'Volksgemeinschaft', or national community. In both Germany and Italy, fascist parties attempted to supervise the birth process, increasing the number of births and decreasing women's control over their own bodies. Third, as Wilhelm Reich pointed out, fascism was a sexualised movement. A large part of its appeal (to both men and women) relied on a visual imagery, which glorified the human body, while remaining resolutely hostile to the representation of sex. Fourth, fascism's hostile attitude towards women's rights was not merely a matter of past history. Neo-nazi and fascist parties in post-war Europe have been equally hostile towards the goals of women's liberation.

In all fairness, Durham could argue that these potential criticisms of his argument are tangential to his central argument, which is that at times women did join the fascist parties. If fascism was so hostile to women, then how could this take place? To answer this point, however, requires going beyond *Women and Fascism*. Insofar as Durham has a theory to explain women's occasional support for fascism, it is simply to repeat the claims of fascists and fascist sympathisers, namely that there was something objectively pro-female about fascism. In his words, 'fascism was not uniformly misogynist'. The alternative explanation is to indicate that (in general terms) people are capable of supporting a movement which is hostile to their interests.

When it comes to questions of economic and social class, the best known theory of 'false consciousness' is the Marxist theory of ideology.

This maintains that at certain times and in a temporary way, people are quite capable of supporting a party or a trend which is hostile to their interests. In the work of Karl Marx himself, the classic example of such an observation is his comment on the role of Christianity: 'Religion is the sigh of the oppressed creature, just as it is the spirit of spiritless conditions. It is the *opium* of the people.'[29] This claim is a dual observation, religion is believed by ordinary people and indeed engages with the alienation that many people feel in their lives; but this belief is partial, and needs to be renewed if it is to be sustained. A parallel claim could be made to explain the position of that minority of women who supported the fascist parties. Although fascism was not in their interests, fascism raises enough important questions for at least some women to find its answers appealing. In contrast to Durham's book, such an argument would be neither controversial nor new.

For the actually existing anti-fascists of the 1970s, however, it was not enough merely to announce that fascism was an anti-feminist ideology, in this sense of the term. Instead, this generation of writers progressed from a general theory of ideology to a much more specific and historical theory of fascism, rooted in Wilhelm Reich's work on sexuality. As such, an explanation was offered for the success of fascism, namely that this movement had a sexualised appeal to women which co-existed with the anti-feminist imperative to drive women into the home. The total impression of fascism which emerges then is of a contradictory movement, which offered young women the chance to worship their leaders, while simultaneously denying them the chance to lead fulfilling lives inside and outside the domestic sphere. This emphasis on the contradictory character of fascism co-existed with an emphasis on the ultimately sexist nature of the movement. To borrow from one of the most common fascist images: in Mussolini and Hitler's states, women could play a role in the crowd, but they were not allowed to appear on the platform.[30] One of the motives of fascism was always to deny women a role as real agents in shaping their own lives.

To conclude, Durham's book, *Women and Fascism*, is striking for the depth of the research and the skill with which the author has developed an argument which he had already begun elsewhere. While his book is perhaps correct to suggest that the historical truth is complex and that fascism sometimes received significant female support, it does not succeed in making the case that fascism was feminist, or possessed an objectively feminist agenda. Indeed, reading his book, it is hard to come to anything but the opposite conclusion. The author's detailed and powerful evidence demonstrates, despite the author's intention, that fascism was fundamentally opposed to the independence of women. To explain the paradox of female support for

Hitler and Mussolini, arguments are needed which Durham does not supply. Here, the anti-fascist literature of the 1930s and 1970s becomes especially valuable. Such writers as Wilhelm Reich and David Widgery, among many others, have attempted to explain fascism's gendered appeal to women. As such their theories offer a more compelling answer to the historian's question of 'Where to Begin?'

Notes

1. D. Renton, *Fascism: Theory and Practice* (London, 1999).
2. See, e.g, S. Cullen, 'Four women for Mosley: women in the British Union of Fascists 1932–1940', *Oral History*, vol.24, no.1, 1996, pp.49–59; for a general critique of Cullen's work, see Renton, *Fascism*, p.2; J. Gottlieb, 'Women and fascism in the East End', *Jewish Culture and History*, vol.1, no.2, 1998, pp.31–47; Julie V. Gottlieb, *Feminine Fascism* (London, 2000).
3. M. Durham, *Women and Fascism* (London and New York, 1998), p.4; also M. Durham, 'Gender and the British Union of Fascists', *Journal of Contemporary History*, vol.27, no.3, 1992, pp.513–29; and M. Durham, 'Women and fascism', *Searchlight*, January 2000.
4. This is precisely the approach of Miriam Poya's study into the gender dynamics of post-revolutionary Iran, *Women, Work and Islamism* (London, 2000).
5. Durham, *Women*, pp.13, 20, 64.
6. A. Alexander, 'Daughters of the century, the politics of women's liberation 1900–1999', in K. Flett and D. Renton (eds), *The Twentieth Century. A century of wars and revolutions?* (London, 2000), pp.54–79.
7. R. Evans, *Comrades and Sisters. Feminism, socialism and pacifism in Europe 1870–1945* (Brighton, 1987), p.13.
8. C. Koonz, *Mothers in the Fatherland. Women, the family and Nazi politics* (London, 1987).
9. V. De Grazia, *How Fascism Ruled Women. Italy 1922–1945* (Berkeley, 1992); L. Caldwell, 'Reproducers of the nation: women and the family in fascist policy', in D. Forgacs (ed.), *Rethinking Italian Fascism. Capitalism, populism and culture* (London, 1986).
10. Durham, *Women*, pp.16, 21, 30, 168, 180.
11. Durham, *Women*, p.110.
12. The classic example of this literature is Tim Mason's two-part study of women and German fascism, T. W. Mason, 'Women in Nazi Germany, Part 1', *History Workshop Journal*, 1, 1976, pp.74–113; and 'Women in Germany, 1925–1940: family, welfare and work: conclusion', *History Workshop Journal*, 2, 1976, pp.5–32.
13. For a chronology of women in the anti-racist movement, D. Renton, 'Can the oppressed unite? Women and anti-fascism in Britain 1977–1982', in C. Barker (ed.), *Conference Proceedings. Alternative futures and popular protests 2000* (Manchester, 2000).
14. Women and Fascism Study Group, *Breeders for Race and Nation. Women and fas-*

cism in Britain today (Birmingham, 1978).
15. Women and Fascism Study Group, *Breeders*, p.3.
16. Holtby has also been cited in S. Rowbotham, *Hidden from History. 300 years of women's oppression and the fight against it* (London, 1974), p.126 and in M. Durham, 'Gender', pp.514–15.
17. Women and Fascism Study Group, *Breeders*, p.22.
18. Big Flame, *Sexuality and Fascism* (London, 1979), pp.5, 13.
19. *Women's Voice*, September 1977.
20. *Women's Voice*, February 1978.
21. L. Toothpaste, 'Sex vs. fascism', cited in Women and Fascism Study Group, *Breeders*, pp.21–2. *Temporary Hoarding* was the magazine of Rock Against Racism, while Rock Against Sexism brought out *Drastic Measures*. Sadly, copies of the latter magazine are rare indeed.
22. 'The Dialectics of Liberation', in D. Widgery, *Preserving Disorder* (London, 1989), pp.110–14, 112.
23. Women and Fascism Study Group, *Breeders*, p.18.
24. W. Reich, *The Mass Psychology of Fascism* (London, 1970), pp.98–103; also W. Reich, The Sexual Revolution (London, 1951 edn).
25. Reich, *Mass Psychology*, p. xii; Women and Fascism Study Group, *Breeders*, p.19. Reich's notion of sexual freedom, what might be called 'Sexual Communism', is elaborated in W. Reich, *The Sexual Revolution* (London, 1955 edn).
26. G. L. Mosse, *Nationalism and Sexuality. Respectability as normal sexuality in modern Europe* (New York, 1985), pp.153–81, 161.
27. K. Theweleit, *Male Fantasies I. Women, floods, bodies, history* (Cambridge, 1987), p.227; *Male Fantasies II. Male bodies. Psychoanalyzing the whiter terror* (Cambridge, 1989). For a recent use of Theweleit's categories, A. King, 'The postmodernity of football hooliganism', *British Journal of Sociology*, vol.48, no.4, 1997, pp.576–93. King is criticised in T. Smith, 'MUFC fans, sex and football violence. A "preferred" postmodern past', *North West Labour History*, 24, 1999/2000, pp.55–69.
28. M. Attwood, *The Handmaid's Tale* (London, 1996). I am grateful to Anne Alexander for this reference.
29. This quote from Marx is taken from 'Contribution to the critique of Hegel's philosophy of law', in K. Marx and F. Engels, *Collected Works: Volume 3* (London, 1975), pp. 3–129, 175–87. There is a useful discussion of Marx's theory of ideology in A. Callinicos, *The Revolutionary Ideas of Karl Marx* (London, 1983), pp.97–100. Reich offers his own understanding of ideology as a 'material force', in Reich, *Mass Psychology*, pp.3–33.
30. The relationship between the leader and the crowd in fascist propaganda is discussed in I. Kershaw, *The 'Hitler Myth'. Image and reality in the Third Reich* (Oxford, 1987). Similar themes also inform M. Stone, *The Patron State. Culture and politics in fascist Italy* (Princeton, 1998).

Fascism, Socialism and the Politics of Gender
A reply

Martin Durham

Anyone questioning the ways in which the relationship between women and fascism has often been seen cannot but be aware that they are stepping into a political minefield. At best, a critic of their work will look carefully at the argument they make, examine the material they draw on and then point out areas where they have missed important sources or made judgements that claim more than the evidence will allow. At worst, the topic will draw the outraged defender of orthodoxy who will respond not by an exacting examination of the evidence (or even an accurate summary of the argument it underpins) but by a reiteration of what they insist must be true. As I propose to demonstrate, David Renton's discussion paper, and specifically his comments on my own work, falls into the latter category. I am grateful for the opportunity not only to accurately restate my argument but to develop it in ways that I hope will be of interest to readers of the journal.

In Renton's account, my 1998 book, *Women and Fascism*, seeks to present fascism as 'a feminist movement' where the very evidence it cites shows that such an interpretation is impossible. Just as we would expect, he argues, Italian fascism sought to restrict women to increasing the country's population while Sir Oswald Mosley's British Union of Fascists was fixated on selective breeding and the denial of women's rights. Other writers, he goes on, have demonstrated the profoundly anti-feminist nature of National Socialism. The Third Reich sought to remove women from the professions, introduced marriage loans conditional on the woman's withdrawal from the labour market and pressured the supposedly 'fit' to produce children for the master race while those women seen as 'unfit' were sterilised or exterminated.[1]

Not only does *Women and Fascism* refuse to accept the anti-feminist nature of classical fascism, Renton argues, it is similarly blind to the misogyny at the heart of post-war fascism. The National Front, for instance, treated women as sexual objects and in looking both at the inter-war and post-war periods, a book which Renton is kind enough to describe as well researched nonetheless deliberately refuses to acknowledge the 'compelling explanation of the relationship between women and fascism' that was advanced by anti-fascist writers over twenty years ago.[2] Such an indictment might appear to some of *Socialist History*'s readers as itself compelling, and any attempt to defend the proposition that fascism should be seen as feminist both impossible and immoral to make. Fortunately, such a task need not be carried out, for the simple reason that I do not believe it to be true and do not argue it in my book. Instead, as I envisaged any reader of my work would readily see, my claim is that it is not at all the case that at all times, and by definition, fascism believes that women's place is in the home, producing children for race and nation. Much of what we know about Mussolini's Italy and Nazi Germany does indeed accord with such a picture.[3] But as Renton dismissively notes, I offer what he calls 'a series of yes–buts', claiming that Italian fascism was not anti-feminist from its inception and that even Nazism was more complex than we assume.[4]

This is indeed the case. In the extended period over which I have constructed what Renton describes as my 'provocative' argument, there were three particular moments in which a conventional understanding of women and classical fascism which I myself assumed to be true were thrown into disarray. The first, which I will return to, was to actually read the publications of the British Union of Fascists, a literature never cited in Renton's critique but which disrupts any simple assumption that the overtly patriarchal views held by many fascists represented the only position on gender espoused within the extreme right. The second moment in which I came to realise that there was something wrong with the orthodoxy Renton attempts to defend was when reading work by the American feminist Leila J. Rupp which revealed not only that the Nazi Party paper had published a debate on women in the mid-1920s but that in 1932, in an effort to strengthen its potential support among working women, the party had issued propaganda material denying it sought to deprive women of their jobs and attempted, however unpersuasively, to 'clarify' some of the more brazenly male chauvinist pronouncements of its leading figures.[5] If it is that article that had the most dramatic effect on my thinking about Nazism, then my assumptions about Italian fascism were similarly shaken by reading extracts from a Mussolini speech to fascist members of the Italian Parliament in 1925 in which he called on them to react favourably to the telegrams from fascist women calling for the vote to be extended to women and to accept that in 'the century of capitalism', women could no longer be denied a place either in the workplace or society.[6] None of this led me to conclude that fascism was inherently feminist. What it did do, however, was to end any belief that it was always openly opposed to women's rights and suggest instead that just as different fascisms have adopted different economic policies, different foreign policies and different stances towards religion and towards biological racism, so there was also a hitherto untraced history of different fascist responses towards the demands of women.

Women and work

In the Italian case, I argue, anti-feminism proved victorious by the late 1920s while the Nazi Party's decision shortly after its formation to forbid women members from standing as electoral candidates was a powerful indication of how strong a male supremacist rendering of fascism was from long before the party came to power. The drive to increase the birth-rate is crucial in understanding the two regimes, as Renton and I agree, as is the preferential treatment given to men in employment. (It would be a mistake, of course, to claim that fascism drove women as a whole from the workplace. Indeed, while Italian fascism considered large-scale expulsion at the end of the 1930s, female employment remained high in Nazi Germany and in the late 1930s the condition that marriage loans were only available if the wife withdrew from paid work was abandoned.)[7] But if anti-feminism was dominant in both German Nazism and Italian fascism, it was not indisputably so, and if we turn to the British Union of Fascists, we find a very different balance of forces.

Where Hitler forbade women Nazis running for office, Mosley emphasised the presence of eleven women among the eighty candidates selected for parliamentary constituencies, and while BUF propagandists sometimes argued that in 'the Greater Britain' they sought, men would once again be the breadwinners and women restored to hearth and home, they also declared that women should choose whether or not to work and that if they did so they would receive equal pay and access to any jobs that they were physically capable of performing.[8] Feminists were mistaken, the leading BUF writer, Alexander Raven Thomson, claimed, to believe fascism sought to restrict women to the production of 'cannon fodder'. Instead, he argued, whether they worked outside the home or not, in the future Corporate State they would be represented by their own sex in greater numbers than they were under democracy.[9]

At times the argument for equal pay was posed in terms of making women less attractive to employers and there is no need and, it might be added, insufficient evidence, to conclude that the BUF genuinely believed in women's equality. Some of its members—or leaders—may well have done so and it is noteworthy, despite the damage it does to his argument, that

Renton describes some women members of the BUF as feminists.[10] What the printed record makes clear, however, is that different views on gender were expressed in BUF publications (as I noted in an earlier article, where one woman member's article was entitled 'Fascism will Mean Real Equality for Women', another declared 'Fascist Women Do Not Want Equal Rights With Men').[11] Even more importantly, some of the party's propaganda and policies were deliberately intended to rebut claims that fascism would deprive women of their rights. Despite Renton's suggestion that such views were those of a minority, I know of no basis to be sure he is right or not. What cannot be in doubt, however, is that since the BUF never came to power, we should put particular weight on what Renton terms 'the ideas which are promulgated'.[12] They were not, I suggest, the ideas that conventional accounts of women and fascism would lead us to expect.

The post-war picture

While much of *Women and Fascism* is concerned with inter-war fascism, it also gives extensive consideration to post-war developments and here too traditional interpretations need to come under criticism. As with the Nazi Party, the National Front of the 1970s was virulently anti-abortion, opposed to feminism and desperately concerned to increase the racial birth-rate. Such views were particularly espoused in the pages of the main publication issued in its support, the monthly magazine *Spearhead*, but, as Renton notes, one could also find a blatant sexism in the Young National Front's magazine, *Bulldog*, in which pictures of young women in NF T-shirts were used to titillate its largely male readership. Contrary to his bizarre misrepresentation of my argument, I did not describe this as proof of the 'sympathetic treatment' that women received in NF publications but instead noted that 'while pictured as sex-objects, this did not mean that women could not play a politically active role'.[13] Nonetheless, we can agree that the NF of the 1970s can most certainly not be described as feminist. But does this mean that it validates the orthodox picture of fascism that he seeks to defend?

You would not know from his account, for instance, that the NF's policy on abortion was disputed within its ranks, with the decision of its Annual General Meeting to condemn the issuing of an anti-abortion election address in the October 1974 election not being reversed until four years later. It was the subject of dispute too on the NF's leading body, the National Directorate, and one of the groups that broke away from the NF as it entered into crisis following the 1979 General Election decided at its founding conference to abandon any anti-abortion policy. The NF itself in the 1980s continued to be strongly anti-abortion, a tradition continued when it split into two warring bands in the mid-1980s, but both experienced internal conflict over the issue.[14]

Nor has the NF spoken with one voice over women's rights more generally. In the 1980s, one prominent male activist published an article criticising the NF's neglect of such issues as unequal pay and sexual harassment and claiming that it was the duty of 'racial nationalists' to defend women's interests as well as men's. The election of two women to the NF's national leadership later in the decade led to the party magazine publishing an interview in which one of them attacked male chauvinism within the NF. As I argued in *Women and Fascism*, tensions over abortion in particular and women's role more generally have also surfaced in the post-war extreme right in other countries.[15] With such unsettling evidence not of the monolithic nature of fascism's relationship to women, but its diversity and disputatiousness, how might we evaluate earlier attempts to understand the gender politics of the extreme right?

Here not only Renton's account of the emergence in the 1970s of a 'compelling' portrayal of the extreme right but my use of the notion of a gravely flawed orthodoxy hit problems. What appears at moments to be a defence of a classical Marxist understanding turns out, on closer examination, to be the advocacy of arguments that neither the Communist International nor the founding generation of Trotskyism would, or could, have accepted. Renton notes that writers of the 1970s drew on an earlier generation of antifascists but instead of, for instance, Dimitrov or Togliatti or Trotsky, he cites the highly heterodox ex-communist Wilhelm Reich and the determinedly non-Marxist Virginia Woolf.[16] Both in the 1970s and forty years earlier, we are plainly engaging with a wide array of different approaches to the issue, and to present them as if they were one united—and wholly persuasive—body of argument does no service to understanding where earlier work proves helpful and where it does not. In the book itself, I did discuss some of the other writers Renton refers to, but somewhat more briefly than I would have wished.[17] The time taken up to discuss women and fascism in Germany, Italy and Britain before the Second World War and in Germany, Italy, France and Britain in more recent decades left little opportunity to address the body of work that Renton recommends to us. If I had done so, however, it would not have led to the same conclusion as he does.

The differences within

Some of the material Renton cites richly deserves re-examination. The Birmingham Centre for Contemporary Cultural Studies pamphlet, for instance, was particularly noteworthy in its use of earlier writers, and in its discussion of Reich was especially useful in criticising both his over-reliance on sexuality as a causal factor in fascism and his homophobic association of the extreme right's attraction to men with gay men's attraction to each other. Both it and the pamphlet by the libertarian socialist grouping Big Flame offered extraordinarily valuable suggestions as to how fascism appealed to its supporters, appeals that included women's fear of crime, mothers' protectiveness towards their children and men's fears that rising unemployment and the decline of industrial work would take away the very core of their lives.[18]

Other material produced during the period was of a different character. In particular, to acknowledge that Women Against the Nazis bravely opposed fascism is not to be confused with believing that it made valuable contributions to our understanding of it, and while it came under fire from some on the left for its anxiety that if the NF came to power, 'We would lose control over our kids', it also demonstrated a peculiar understanding of the subject in its claim that a victorious British fascism would ban kissing in public. [19]

But if we are arguing not for the unanimity of 1970s anti-fascist writings but its unevenness, in one area it was in agreement. At its best, it documented what the Nazis had done to women and how *Spearhead* perceived them. What it did not do, however, was prove that fascism as such must always so act or so believe. Ironically, one of the publications Renton celebrates, *Women's Voice*, did publicise details of the NF's division on abortion when, in 1979, it printed a letter which cited the entire text of the resolution for the 1979 National Front Annual General Meeting calling for the organisation to officially oppose abortion. Yet even with the leaking of such a document, the letter-writer merely took this protest at the NF's reluctance to condemn abortion as proof that fascism opposed women's rights. [20]

As with Renton's reference to feminists within the BUF, so with *Women's Voice* long before, the assumption that fascism is always overtly anti-feminist appears impervious to the very evidence that is cited. A closer examination of anti-fascist writings than either I or he has engaged in is likely to produce further instances where the supposed uniformity of fascism's gender politics has been cast into doubt. The *Daily Worker*, for example, once published details of an exchange in the British Union of Fascists press as to whether fascism was or was not genuine as to its claims to accept women's rights and an even more intriguing example is to be found in the left's treatment of one of the most unsettling cases of all, the existence of a grouping in the early years of the Third Reich which condemned Nazi policies as denying Aryan women their rightful equality. Hilary Newitt's 1937 Victor Gollancz book compared 'the position of women' in the Soviet Union, western democracies and under fascism. Discussing the last, she cited material from the August, September and October 1933 issues of 'the women's paper, *Die Deutsche Kämpferin*'. The first had contained a letter from two women, one a Nazi, the other a member of its ultra-conservative ally, the German National People's Party, who had been dismissed from their posts as welfare managers on grounds of sex. The second of the issues had noted the sacking of women headteachers; the third, women's removal from the Prussian Health Committee. While Newitt did not explain the political provenance of the publication she had drawn on, another Communist Party publication of the period did. In *Women Under Fascism and Communism*, Hilda Browning cited the same paper denouncing the exclusion of women from the funeral of the former German President, Hindenberg, and condemning the denial of women's right to work and attempts to make them 'play the part of breeding cattle'. Nowhere, the paper declared, 'do we find a divine or natural law allowing one of the sexes to claim all the pleasant, honourable, well-paid and leading positions for itself, and leaving the menial, hard and badly-paid jobs to the other'. Such sentiments could indeed be cited favourably in an anti-fascist publication—but who, when Hitler had banned the publications of the left, was making such arguments? Browning noted that a group of Nazi women had published an address to Hitler, declaring that 'For decades now women have been waking to a new consciousness' and that they were now 'being sacrificed to the irresponsibility of the men' who had allowed nationalists to come to power who refused to accept women's equality. Finally Browning closed the circle. Citing the German paper's attack on the new regime's 'un-Nordic' treatment of prostitutes as 'a marketable commodity' for men, Browning revealed that *Die Deutsche Kämpferin* had issued a 'challenge...by the National Socialist women'. Indeed, as later writers have discussed, the paper and the address to Hitler represented an effort by extreme right-wing women to attack the Nazi policy towards women as incompatible with true German racism.[21] Over sixty years ago, an anti-fascist publication could acknowledge the existence of differences among fascists on gender. It is a shame that that insight has not persisted.

Calculation and conflict

If, as I have sought to demonstrate, fascism is not invariably anti-feminist, why should this be so? In addition to mistakenly claiming that I see fascism as feminist, Renton also claims somewhat inconsistently that my 'central argument' is 'that at times women did join the fascist parties'.[22] This, of course, would hardly be a distinctive (or controvertible) claim, and his assertion that my only explanation for such a phenomenon is that there is 'something objectively pro-female about fascism' represents another misreading of my argument.[23] If, as I claim, there is no single relationship between fascism and gender, then I also claim there is no single explanation for fascism's appeal. One of my criticisms of Reich is that he says very little about fascism's specific appeal to women and I have also been unpersuaded by the arguments of one of the other writers cited by Renton, the post-war Italian communist Maria-Antoinetta Macciocchi.[24] One suggestion that I have found particularly intriguing is that made in a French feminist publication that the *Front National* speaks in different ways to women, addressing those in the older generation nostalgic for Vichy France in different tones from the more modern, younger racist voters.[25] I do not disagree here with Renton's suggestion that fascist arguments have important points of contact with those of conservatism (although here we would need to explain why fascism tends to be much stronger among men while conservatism has historically had a strong appeal to women).[26] But if I could (and perhaps should) have said more about how fascism appeals to both men and women, I do believe that it is already possible to explain the very differences within fascism that my work has emphasised and Renton is at pains to deny.

In part, we need to be sensitive to national traditions, that women are seen differently in particular national cultures. But there are also two crucial factors that impact on fascism more broadly. The first is to do with electoral calculation. If even the Nazis sought to deny their antagonism to women's right to work, we should not be surprised if, in pursuit of the maximum popular support, extreme right parties would not wish to risk alienating those who share their views on race and nation but do not believe that women's place is in the home. The second factor, as we have seen, is that people with just those reservations—or convictions—can be members and not just potential supporters, and a struggle can break out within fascist parties as to what exactly their stance on abortion or women and work should be. The result of such calculation and such conflict is likely to present grave problems for those who seek to understand fascism. If those within the extreme right who loathe feminism and are antagonistic to calls for sexual freedom are likely to defeat challenges from others within their movement, this is not pre-ordained. Despite Renton's fears, there is no threat to anti-fascism in acknowledging the different forms which fascism takes, and the tensions which exist within its ranks. It is here, rather than in the pretence that fascism can only take one stance on gender that, to borrow Renton's closing image, we should begin.

Notes

1. David Renton, 'Women and Fascism', *Socialist History*, 20, pp.72–83
2. Renton, 'Women and Fascism', this issue.
3. Martin Durham, *Women and Fascism* (London, 1998), p.4.
4. Renton, 'Women and Fascism', this issue.
5. Leila J. Rupp, 'Mother of the Volk. The image of women in Nazi ideology', *Signs*, 3.2,1977, pp.364–6; *Mobilizing Women for War. German and American propaganda* (Princeton, 1978), pp.18–26.
6. Donald Meyer, *Sex and Power. The rise of women in America, Russia, Sweden and Italy* (Middletown, CT, 1989), p.28.
7. Durham, *Women*, pp.167–8, 14, 25–6.
8. O. Mosley, *Tomorrow We Live* (London, 1938), p.16; Durham, *Women*, pp.30–8, 59.
9. Durham, *Women*, pp.31–2.
10. Renton, 'Women and Fascism', this issue.
11. Martin Durham, 'Women and the British Union of Fascists, 1932–1940', *Immigrants and Minorities*, vol. 8, nos 1–2, 1989, p.8.
12. Renton, 'Women and Fascism, this issue.
13. Renton, 'Women and Fascism', this issue; Durham, *Women*, p.110.
14. Durham, *Women*, pp.136–42.
15. Durham, *Women*, pp.152–3, 111–12, 86, 178.
16. Renton, 'Women and Fascism', this issue.
17. Durham, *Women*, pp.166, 175–6, 180.
18. Women and Fascism Study Group, *Breeders for Race and Nation* (Birmingham, n.d., c.1979), pp.15, 18–20; Big Flame, *Sexuality and Fascism* (reprinted London, 1991), pp.13–14.
19. *Women and the Nazis* (London, 1978), n.p.; *Socialist Press*, 25 October 1978.
20. *Women's Voice*, March 1979.
21. *Daily Worker*, 7 April 1934; Hilary Newitt, *Women Must Choose* (London, 1937), cover, pp.52–4, 271; Hilda Browning, *Women Under Fascism and Communism* (London, n.d., c.1935), pp.16–17, 20–1.
22. Renton, 'Women and Fascism', this issue.
23. Renton, 'Women and Fascism', this issue.
24. Durham, Women, pp.175–6; for a discussion of two other writers cited by Renton, Winifred Holtby and Klaus Thewelheit, see pp.175–6, 180.
25. O. Mericourt, 'L'Extreme droite en France. Enfants, cuisine, eglise (Kinder, Kuche, Kirche)', *Les Cahiers du Feminisme*, 54, 1990.
26. Renton, 'Women and fascism', this issue.

Reviews

Books to be remembered (3)

Bert Birtles, *Exiles in the Aegean. A personal narrative of Greek politics and travel* (London, 1938)

The turbulent politics of Greece during the years between the two world wars were not widely commented on within British radical groups. There was a growing interest in the closing years of the 1930s but Spain and Nazi Germany naturally were still the central areas of political concern. During the war and the immediate post-war years Greece was to become an important country in the debates and conflicts that were to be repeated continuously for the next half century.

This present book was published in the summer of 1938 by the Left Book Club, not as one of their monthly titles that went to all members but as an additional volume which could be purchased. The author, Bert Birtles, an Australian journalist, was making his first visit to Europe. He had been in Palestine on a journalistic survey and came to Greece for a holiday with his wife Dora who had been away from Australia for some three years. It was not Birtles's original intention to report on any aspect of the Greek situation.

Books on Greek politics in the twentieth century are not in short supply. The usefulness of this present volume is not only its discussion of the politics of 1935 and 1936, although there is much that will interest the historian given the return of the monarchy and the installation of the Metaxas dictatorship, but the detailed account of the lives of political exiles. The Greek courts would often hand down sentences to those whom they decided were political dissidents which combined prison and exile. Exile would mean so many months or years on one of the many islands in the Aegean, and the middle section of this book tells of an eight-day visit to the island of Anaphi by Birtles and his wife. It was understood to be one of the worst of its kind.

Political dissidents—there were 35 during the Birtles visit—were given ten drachmas a day (equivalent to five pence in English money at the time). At this time the Red Cross were sending a further five drachmas to each exile. From this allowance they had to buy water, all their food, and pay for the rent of their accommodation. If the local police were of the opinion, rightly or wrongly, that any one individual had a private income, of whatever size, the money allowance was withheld.

The first duty Greek communists 'imposed' on themselves, in exile or in prison, was the formation of a collective. Its purposes were to protect or limit the degree of maltreatment; to ensure a proper organisation of duties needed to encourage as civilised an existence as was practicable; to arrange for the fair distribution of what were always meagre supplies of food; and to adjudicate in the event of serious differences between individuals or groups. If there were ten or more, in prison or in exile, a secretary would be elected along with a storekeeper and a treasurer. Every month a general meeting was held at which the past weeks' living conditions were reviewed, and problems and grievances were debated.

Newcomers to the collective were informed of the procedures expected of them and it was made clear that the rules were strict. Not all the members of collectives were communists but all political exiles were encouraged to join. There were some matters considered essential. All the islands—even the most desolate—always seemed to have some peasants, mostly in villages, and there were very firm rules concerning the relations between the collective and the local peasants. Especially the women. It was specifically laid down that there must be no advances to any of the local women and no sexual relations. It was explained to the Birtles that the peasantry were 'backward' and that any involvement with the peasant women might well encourage retribution from the husband or the family, and that the collective itself might be damaged. What is especially notable was the care the collective took in the administration of discipline. Here is an extract from the account of how the monthly meetings were organised:

> Every member has the right to make proposals for ameliorating conditions and anybody who has not been abiding by the rules is told about it—he may not have been thorough enough at his job, whether it was cleaning dishes or sweeping rooms, or he may not have attended his study circle, or again, he may have acted towards police or peasants in a way the collective considered unwise. The group's disapproval is the only punishment. During the month nothing is said to an offender and at the meeting harsh words are not used. The hope is merely expressed that it will be the last time he will have to appear before the meeting for

lack of discipline, and the comrades assured us that they found this very effective.

The Birtles, back in Athens and other parts of Greece talked to many who had been in exile and their accounts provide a detailed review of living and working conditions. There were a large number who were quite certain that without the organisation the collective provided many more deaths would have occurred. It was accepted that living conditions were such that for a majority health was always undermined and illnesses of various kind were always the result. For all in a collective, education was compulsory and given the high rate of illiteracy among the peasantry and working people in general, the provision of classes of different kinds and levels was accepted as a major responsibility of the collective's organisation.

The most interesting social problem was probably the relationships between men and women. Given the traditions of a peasant society deeply engraved in the masculine personality, the difficulties the communists had in explaining what a socialist relationship between the sexes involved were not easily resolved. The discipline within the collective was not difficult to understand but for many from the villages the social relationship between the sexes had to be learned, and it was not easy. Women who were party members had learned. Birtles discussed the question with one of the two women in the collective on Anaphi, both of whom were communist:

> 'What did she mean exactly by the rights of women?... I mean the same political and economic rights as men, I mean freedom from having to work in the house, and freedom from having to care for children. I want to see mechanical laundries established, communal restaurants, creches, and I want legislation to provide for maternity protection, social protection for children, equal pay for women and men, equal work, and equality in political representation also, and the right to sit in Parliament. Women should have equal opportunity with men to rise to any position. They should also be given equal education. Girls should be given social protection, not just the protection of their parents. They should be able to become whatever they most want to be. A girl might want to be an architect, an engineer or a mechanic. If so, the way should be open to her.
>
> Have you got these ideas from what you have heard or read about Russia? No...These ideas grew gradually in my mind from the life I led. Now I have found out that they are actually in force in the life that women lead in Russia.

These words were spoken in 1935; a truly remarkable statement. We may ignore the reference to Russia since these were common beliefs in the middle of the 1930s among communists the world over. It is the recital of women's rights and the relations between men and women that is so impressive, and it came out of a society brutalised by poverty and semi-fascist authoritarianism.

The literature on Greece during the Second World War is voluminous with this book by Birtles being absent from most accounts. Yet the description of the Resistance organisation which by the end of 1944 controlled almost all Greece outside the big and some medium-sized cities relates directly to the experience of the political exiles that Birtles set down in this 1938 volume. It is to be regretted that it has not been more widely used, a statement that must also recognise the excellent and erudite scholarship that has given us the heroic story of the Greek resistance.[1]

John Saville
Professor emeritus, University of Hull

Note

1. Marion Sarafis was an Englishwoman who first went to Greece before the Second World War as an archaeologist where she met her future husband. After the war, in the later 1940s, they married. Her husband, an Army officer by the name of Stefanos Sarafis, became the military leader of ELAS and died in 1957 from a motor-car accident almost certainly 'arranged' by the American CIA. In 1946 Sarafis wrote a lengthy account of his wartime activities, since fully translated into English (*ELAS. Greek Resistance Army*, Merlin Press, 1980). Sarafis also edited papers from a conference at the LSE in 1978 (*Greece. From resistance to civil war*, Spokesman Books, 1980). This is an important book since the participants in the conference came from different positions within the Greek political and military wartime movements. Among the many books published on the years of war Mark Mazower, *Inside Hitler's Greece. The experience of occupation 1941–44* (New Haven and London, 1993) offers an erudite and well-written detailed history with a very full bibliography.

Culture in the Cold War

E.P. Thompson *Collected Poems*, edited by Fred Inglis (Bloodaxe Books, Tarset, 1999), 128pp., ISBN 1 85224 422 4, £8.95 pbk.

Historian, critic, essayist, editor, novelist, polemicist and pamphleteer—Edward Thompson was one of the greatest English prose writers of the twentieth century. That he did not write more poetry is hardly surprising, although this was clearly a life-long frustration for Thompson.

These poems certainly feel as though they were written in the margins, on the edge of a passionate life of campaigns and controversies, small pamphlets and large histories. 'In Praise of Hangmen' first turned up in the middle of *The Poverty of Theory*, six of these poems appeared in *The Heavy Dancers*, while 'Infant and Emperor' began life in 1956, grew into a Christmas card in 1961 and was later published as an END pamphlet. The earliest poems are taken from the Kingswood School magazine, written when Thompson was just sixteen and full of half-digested Hopkins, Auden and Rex Warner. Others are culled from letters written in Italy during the war, sounding variously like John Cornford ('and there's no seed of time for us to grudge our loss/ if fiercer knowing, larger love will follow what our fighting does') Day Lewis ('Get up, man, stand up, stand, you Englishman!') and Edward Thomas ('And Englishmen/are fighting at Cassino for such lanes as these').

There are individual poems here of great concentrated power and beauty, particularly the half-dozen love poems for his wife Dorothy published here for the first time. No future anthology of Second World War verse will be able to ignore poems like 'Casola Valsenio' and 'Approach March, Last Offensive'. And few poets ever wrote so well about the foul culture of nuclear weapons as Thompson did in 'The Place Called Choice' and 'Infant and Emperor'. He was, as Fred Inglis says in his introduction to this remarkable book, '*the* writer of the Cold War'.

Unfortunately, Inglis never explains what this means (and for younger readers the Cold War is going to take some explaining). His claim that Thompson was exceptional because—unlike the rest of the British left—he did not have 'tin ears and concrete ideologies' needs *explaining* to readers who will not remember the brief and bizarre influence of Louis Althusser on the academic left in Britain. Milton, Swift, Blake, Wordsworth, Yeats and Auden *may* have been Thompson's 'literary masters' but this tells us nothing about Thompson's poetry. (And Inglis is surely wrong to include in this list Eliot, a writer whom Thompson hated.)

More useful would have been some discussion of the poems in their immediate contexts. Like all occasional poems, they were shaped by the events to which they tried to respond. 'The Place Called Choice,' for example, was written for the 1951 Festival of Britain competition (and of course rejected by the culture of 'pious pus' which the poem opposes). Thompson's early poems might have benefited from some mention of Arnold Rattenbury and Geoffrey Matthews, comrades at Kingswood (and later) in both politics and poetry. Although half these poems were written while Thompson was an active member of the Communist Party, there is no discussion of the Salisbury Group, where communist writers—including Thompson—met in the late 1940s, or of his poetry reviewing in the *Daily Worker* in the early

1950s (the only period when he wrote regularly about contemporary poetry). Inglis tells us that Thompson admired John Berryman and Ted Hughes (though there is no evidence of this in his poetry) but says nothing of communist poets who did influence Thompson like Edgell Rickword, Hamish Henderson and Randall Swingler ('Infant and Emperor' owes a good deal to Swingler's Christmas oratorio *The Winter Journey*).

This is perhaps connected to the omission of several of Thompson's communist poems, like 'A Vision of Eden' (first published in *Poetry Broadsheets*) 'John Bull's Christmas', and 'New Year, 1948', first published in *Our Time* (which Thompson helped turn into an aggressive anti-American, Cold War magazine) asking how long must History 'squat upon its heels and wait/ another Lenin on some other star ?' The version of 'The Massacre of the Innocents' published here has lost its roll-call of Cold War villains—liberals, priests, MacArthur, Chiang-Kai-Chek, Syngman Rhee—since first appearing in Communist *Arena*. And there is no room for the splendid 'Trafalgar Square (May Day, 1951)', first published in Emile Burns' Zhdanovite *Daylight*:

> All the Queen's mounted thugs, and all
> The wigs in Westminster could not
> Keep William Morris from this spot
> Not staunch the clams of Alf Linnell.
> But still the killers of Linnell
> Straddle the carpetbagger's State,
> Provoking the crowds to meditate
> How much more serene and beautiful
> The beasts below than those above,
> Who mass behind the Bishop's prayer
> Their squads of moral hoof and hair,
> And—while the liberals cry "love"—
> Within the barracks oil their guns.
> Comrades, forget it to you cost
> Our Bloody Sunday's always lost
> The day the workers think it's won :
> But each year that we march presages
> The day we square accounts, the day
> The peasants take the land for pay
> The workers draw the world in wages,
> When from Mile End to Leningrad
> We come into the streets for good—
> Not all the banners we can hold

Will match the pealing of our blood.
While the riderless horses of the police
Draw past the pageants of human peace.

This is all very unfortunate, since it minimises the extent to which Thompson himself was, before 1956, a Cold Warrior. So much of the force of Thompson's writings against the Cold War derived from the fact that he had previously inhabited its Manichean geography (and how many writers from Natopolis ever rebelled against the Cold War's toxic 'contagion'?) For Thompson, the forces of the Herod state ('Horseman and eagles, Emperor, wolf and bull') never belonged to one side only, nor did they spring fully armed from the soil only in 1945. As these poems testify, the world was swallowed by 'the worm of power' long before then. The Cold War may be over, but still the world lies curled within its poisonous coils.

Andy Croft
Freelance writer and poet

Randall Swingler, *Selected Poems*, edited by Andy Croft (Trent Editions, Nottingham, 2000), xxii+111pp., ISBN 1 84233 014 4, £7.99 pbk.

Between 1933 and 1956 fifty or more poets were members of the Communist Party. Most were very minor figures, but at least a dozen wrote verse of real distinction. After years of neglect, there are welcome signs of a revival of interest in their work. The collected poems of Edward Thompson and Jack Beeching have recently been published, and this selection from Randall Swingler's work, with a useful biographical introduction, should make a remarkable poet's work known to a wider public.

In many respects Swingler was typical of the communist poets of his generation, most of whom had a middle-class background and a university education. Born in 1909, the son of a country parson, he was educated at Winchester and Oxford, and joined the party in 1934, when the depression, the spread of Fascism and the threat of war were influencing many intellectuals to take this step. As journalist, critic, editor, playwright and publisher he gave devoted service to the party, while keeping up a steady output of both propagandist verse and more ambitious poetry. One of his political songs, 'Sixty Cubic Feet', is a little masterpiece, but most of this agitprop is of merely historical interest, and could have been spared from this selection to leave room for more important work. He served in the Army from 1941 to 1946, mostly in North Africa and Italy, and was awarded the Military Medal for bravery.

His last two collections, *The Years of Anger* (1946) and *The God in the Cave*

(1950), form the nucleus of the selection. The former brings together examples of his pre-war verse and the series of poems that he wrote while serving on the Italian front. They are the poems of a sensitive man torn between his loathing of war and his conviction of the justice of the allied cause:

> If we live—But I who live by my love.
> And by my love create, feel, know,
> Must enter this region where love cannot go,
> Must in this moment be what most I hate
> And yet because it is my love which here I negate,
> Because this instant's life is the knowledge of death,
> Because we handle fate like a Bren gun and have learned to hate,
> Life is assured, and some world will be saved.

Although both the Army and the party urged him to apply for a commission, he preferred to remain in the ranks, apart from being promoted to corporal. He was thus able to speak for the common soldier in his poems, which stand among the most powerful that the war produced, with those of Keith Douglas and Hamish Henderson. *The God in the Cave* consists of two sequences in which he attempts, not altogether successfully, to come to terms with the post-war world. Lacking the conviction that sustained him at the front, they are even more painful reading than his war poems. In only one of his poems, 'The Possible', does he mention the USSR. However idealised their mental picture of the Soviet regime, the communist poets wrote little verse about it. One of the few exceptions, Cecil Day Lewis's 'On The Twentieth Anniversary of Soviet Power', describes the USSR as 'the vision's proof, the lifting of despair', and Swingler similarly tells himself, if tempted to despair, that 'already the lands live, where…all we fight for, is already growing'. To the poets, as to most communists, the USSR was a comforting myth.

Although Swingler lost his faith at Oxford, he remained profoundly influenced by his Christian upbringing. Croft suggests that he joined the party 'via Lawrence, Blake and the New Testament'. Among the other communist poets, Edgell Rickword, Christopher Caudwell, Hugh MacDiarmid, Montagu Slater, Arnold Rattenbury, Jack Beeching, Geoffrey Matthews and the brothers Frank and Edward Thompson all came from a religious background, whether Anglican, Catholic, Presbyterian, or Methodist. Some of them found in the Bible a source of poetic mythology, as when Day Lewis and MacDiarmid used the flood story as a symbol of revolution. The first sequence in *The God in the Cave* sees the returning soldier as Lazarus risen from the grave, a reminiscence of Swingler's own experience in 1943, when his signal unit was buried alive by enemy shelling and he was the only survivor. In 'The Winter Journey' and 'Carol' he drew on the nativity stories in the Gospels as symbols of regeneration, as Edward Thompson did in his sequence 'Infant and Emperor'. The influence of Christianity on British Communism would repay study.

In the post-war years Swingler found himself, in Croft's words, 'victimised by both McCarthyism and Zhdanovism'. His writings were rejected by editors, publishers and the BBC, and a magazine which he edited closed down when the backer discovered that he was a Communist. His treatment by the little Zhdanovs of King Street was no better. He and Rickword were forced to resign their joint editorship of the cultural monthly *Our Time*. A series which he launched of shilling poetry booklets, including *The God in the Cave* and books by four other Communists and five non-Communists, was attacked in the *Daily Worker* as 'the musty blowings of an obscure and unintelligible clique', and a projected second series had to be abandoned.

When Khrushchev's report on Stalin's crimes revealed that the British party leadership had been lying to the members for twenty years, Swingler resigned. After the Soviet invasion of Hungary, the British leadership's attempt to defend it and the adoption of a document on 'inner-party democracy', most of the remaining writers followed his example. The ultimate issue was truth, a value as fundamental to the poets, whom Wilfred Owen had reminded that 'the true Poets must be truthful', as to the historians and scientists who resigned with them.

The eleven years that remained to Swingler were darkened by depression, poverty and ill health, yet he still occasionally produced poems that rank among his best. It is to be hoped that this selection will encourage a publisher to bring out a fuller collection, as well as Croft's unpublished biography of a fine poet and brave man.

Charles Hobday
author of *Edgell Rickword: A Poet at War (Carcanet Press, Manchester, 1989)*

Tony Shaw, *British Cinema and the Cold War. The State, Propaganda and Consensus* (IB Tauris, London and New York, 2001), xii+282pp., ISBN 1 8606 437 1, £39.50 hbk.

For those of us who lived through the Cold War for most of our adult lives it is somewhat disconcerting to find that it is already a suitable subject for younger generations of historians. This is nonetheless a welcome development when the historical scholarship is of such consistently high quality as that of this particular monograph.

Tony Shaw sets out to examine the impact of Cold War attitudes and preconceptions on British cinema in what he terms the 'first Cold War', from the late 1940s to the early 1960s. The dust jacket rightly describes this period as 'the last phase of cinema's dominance as a mass entertainment form in Britain'. In later phases of the Cold War cinema yielded pride of place to television as a mass entertainment medium and therefore also as the preferred channel for propaganda aimed at the mass audience. This was the age before spin-doctoring was quite as openly practised as it is today and when Reithian notions of balance and objectivity had not yet been seriously questioned, if not undermined.

The advantages of television over cinema have been well rehearsed elsewhere but one clear advantage of cinema over television (at least from the propagandist's point of view) is that it has always been, and remains essentially a *mass collective experience*. In recognising the potential of this characteristic Soviet agitprop experts were ahead of their colleagues elsewhere and Shaw neatly and convincingly portrays the ways in which respect for and awe before the classic canon of Soviet cinema influenced British film-makers and politicians alike. Fear of the revolutionary potential of even silent Soviet cinema meant that Eisenstein's *The Battleship Potemkin* remained banned for public exhibition in the United Kingdom until 1954.

Shaw carefully examines the parallel processes of financial consolidation within the film industry and the growing realisation within government of the need to influence, if not actually control, attitudes towards the new enemy in the East through the information flow provided by entertainment cinema. The book contains ample evidence that the Society for Cultural Relations with the USSR, a communist front organisation, had its countervailing equivalent in the government's Information Research Division. This will not surprise those who believe that the great unwritten history of the twentieth century is the history of propaganda, but it is encouraging to have our preconceptions confirmed by a work of such meticulous scholarship.

This is the main thrust of the introductory chapter. The second chapter, 'Deviants and Misfits', examines the film treatment of 'the enemy within', those who, in Attlee's words in 1950, 'would stop at nothing to injure our economy and our defence'. Shaw argues convincingly that there was a direct line of continuity from the spy thrillers of the 1930s, such as Hitchcock's *The 39 Steps* (1935) and *The Lady Vanishes* (1938), through wartime features to Victor Saville's *Conspirator*, released in August 1949. While Shaw is surely right to argue that this was 'Britain's first identifiable Cold War feature film', he does in my view underestimate the significance of the Cold War as *background* to Carol Reed's *The Third Man* (1949). But his argument that wartime 'siege conditions' continued, and facilitated anti-Soviet, as opposed to anti-

Nazi propaganda is well made. The chapter traces the development of the spy film through to the Bond movies of the 1960s and demonstrates the significant change in attitudes evidenced by such downbeat thrillers as *The Spy Who Came in From the Cold* and *The Ipcress File* (both 1965).

Chapter 3 examines British cinema's depiction of the enemy without. Here the argument is double-pronged. Shaw traces the image of Communism furnished by British film-makers (as, for instance, in Carol Reed's *The Man Between* [1953] or Peter Grenville's *The Prisoner* [1955]) and compares the way in which this image was confirmed or challenged by imported East European films. The distribution of these imported films was of course tightly controlled, so that challenging (or subversive) views were not widely available. What was released often tended to confirm the officially promoted imagery of Communism as an unmitigated totalitarian disaster.

Chapter Four examines the film adaptations of George Orwell's *Animal Farm* (1954) and *Nineteen Eighty-Four* (1956). This is a fascinating chapter and Shaw is right to claim that these two films confirm 'the importance of British, and European, cinema as a forum for the international cultural Cold War' (p.114). Chapter 5 covers the treatment of nuclear warfare and its possible consequences from *Night Boat to Dublin* and *Lisbon Story* (both 1946) to the rather different approaches of Stanley Kubrick's masterly black comedy *Dr Strangelove, or How I learned to Stop Worrying and Love the Bomb* (1964) and Peter Watkins' *The War Game* (1965), which was banned by the BBC on the grounds that it might upset people because, as officials admitted, it demonstrated rather too accurately what might actually happen in Britain after a nuclear attack.

Chapter 6 deals with the depiction of industrial relations on the British Cold War screen, complicated by the desire of some film-makers to inject greater realism into their treatment of everyday life. Here Shaw examines such key films as Alexander Mackendrick's *The Man in the White Suit* (1951) for Ealing and the Boulting brothers' controversial *I'm All Right Jack* (1959), contrasting them with the later approach found in the film adaptations of Alan Sillitoe's two novels, *Saturday Night and Sunday Morning* and *The Loneliness of the Long-Distance Runner*, both made in the early 1960s. The final chapter examines the films that challenged the consensus directly or indirectly, some through the employment of those who had been blacklisted by Hollywood at its McCarthyite nadir such as Charlie Chaplin (*A King in New York* [1956]) or Joseph Losey (*The Damned* [1961]). Shaw also discusses the impact of East European films such as Mikhail Chiaureli's *The Fall of Berlin* (1949), the apotheosis of the 'cult of personality' and therefore, in the Foreign Office's view 'too obviously one-sided to be effective communist propaganda for British audiences'. It is hardly surprising therefore that this was also 'perhaps the most widely seen of all Soviet-made Second World War films imported into Britain in the 1940s and 1950s' (both p.187).

Tony Shaw has produced a fascinating study and an excellent piece of scholarship. He has given his readers an impressively nuanced account of the ways in which British cinema during the 'first Cold War', while it might not have told audiences what to think, certainly directed them towards what they should think about.

Richard Taylor
University of Wales, Swansea

A Radical Education

Geoff Andrews, **Hilda Kean** and **Jane Thompson** (eds), *Ruskin College: Contesting Knowledge, Dissenting Politics* (Lawrence and Wishart, London, 1999), ISBN 0 85315 899 1, 185pp., £13.99 pbk.

Tony Blair has said his priority is 'Education. Education. Education'. But what kind of education, for whom and for what, is not necessarily clear.

In *Ruskin College: Contesting Knowledge, Dissenting Politics* Jane Thompson makes clear her answers to these questions. Her chapter 'Can Ruskin Survive', starting with the centenary celebrations on 20 February 1999, is a fascinating historical review of the controversies at Ruskin surrounding the 'purpose and nature of education in relation to working-class people. This debate continues in the new fragmented, concealed and more complicated context of the present'. She makes clear where she stands in this debate. 'Widening educational participation will not solve class oppression. Individual solutions do not solve the problems of class relations in capitalism'.

The editors write in the introduction: 'We do not here outline what direction Ruskin should take. If this collection raises questions, creates knowledge and provokes debate it will have served a purpose—of engaging anew with ideas and of continuing a tradition firmly established within Ruskin of contesting knowledge within a framework of political activity and dissent.'

The introduction sets out today's dilemmas for the college. The difficulty of recruiting working class students with no financial resources; perceptions of the purpose of the college; changes in subjects pre-occupying students today, for example, green politics, feminism and post feminism, discrimination and the law. Compare this with the subjects for the Oxford University Diploma in Economics and Political Science in which students were examined when I was at Ruskin (1957–9): economic theory, economic organisation, political history, economic history, political theory and an optional subject. There was also a social workers' course, and a literature course. Grants came from local authorities, scholarships from the college itself, trades unions, the Labour Party, and for miners, the National Coal Board. Now there are financial problems which the Government, with its priorities on education, education, education, should solve.

Ruskin's purpose seemed clear to me. To give workers an education which they would use to help social and economic change beneficial to the working class. Visiting lecturers included leading trades unionists and heads of trade union education departments. Ruskin used the university tutorial system, students meeting their tutors to read their essays and battle it out for an hour. At Ruskin I learned that preaching is not teaching. It was not the brain washing establishment that many on the political left considered it to be.

The truth is more complex. Many left wing activists moved to the right without having ever been near Ruskin. These activists were held to be responsible for their changed opinions. But if a left wing activist went to Ruskin and then moved to the right, it was the college that was held to be responsible. In fact there were left wingers who went to Ruskin and continued to be left wing.

The Ruskin experience did undoubtedly change students' perceptions. Returning to the factory floor after two years at Ruskin posed severe problems as examples in this book illustrate. The political theory lecturer Jay Blumler, ran a research project asking newly arrived students to fill in a form which asked them their reason for going to Ruskin and what they intended to do when they left. They were asked to fill in the same form at the end of their two years. I don't see any reference to this research in the book. Many of the students went on to university, others into jobs in the labour movement, teaching, social work, but I believe in most cases always with the same intentions towards economic and social reform that inspired them before they went to Ruskin.

Bob Purdie was a student in 1974–6. In his chapter 'Ruskin, Student Radicalism, and Civil Rights in Northern Ireland' he gives an interesting account of the students' extra-mural activities in defence of democracy around the world, including the issue of civil rights in Northern Ireland. But I find his account of the NI civil rights movement, detailed as it is, inadequate, particularly in reference to the activities of People's Democracy (PD).

Paul Martin's chapter has a section on music: Reggae, Soul, Rock an' Roll,

Jazz, Funk, Punk. Times change, I accept that, but I find it disappointing that there is no reference to skiffle, folk, and the groups that Jay Blumler organised each year, and the recordings which they made.

In the concluding chapter 'The Place of Ruskin in its Own History' Hilda Kean writes of plans to consolidate Ruskin on its Walton Street site. Perhaps with Ruskin now providing one-year instead of two-year courses this makes sense. But I think they should go back to the two year courses.

There are references to Raphael Samuel and to the History Workshop movement for which he was responsible. The Buxton Hall in which the first Women's Liberation Conference was held in 1970 has been renamed to commemorate his memory. CND was the big issue in my time. The college then had a delegation from Czech trade union colleges and sent a delegation there. It also had links with Kivukoni college in Tanganyika.

To Jane Thompson's question 'Can Ruskin Survive?' I can only say that I think the need for Ruskin, with its social conscience, is as great as ever.

Bert Ward
was a student at Ruskin College from 1957–59

Women's Suffrage

June Purvis and **Sandra Stanley Holton** (eds), *Votes for Women* (Routledge, London and New York, 2000), ISBN 0 415 21459 9, 297pp., £16.99pbk.

There are no full stops to history; the journey never ends, the exploration shifts with the changing times. The idea sometimes mooted by certain historians that there is a sufficient extant literature on the women's suffrage movement, a period which literally furnished a revolution for women, conveys no credibility. *Votes for Women* confirms that the field is gravid with stirring possibilities for feminist historians.

Under the editorship of two such eminent historians, June Purvis and Sandra Stanley Holton, a collection of stimulating research has been garnered from a group of writers recognised in their field. The collection's twelve essays range across several themes. These include the possibility of interpretive realignments nourished by developing discourses such as citizenship; research which focuses on areas of evident neglect as in working-class women's participation and regional activism; the interrogation of extant material to disclose fresh perspectives on issues with a contemporary currency, for instance, the cultural significance of the women's suffrage movement; and finally, the exploration of biographical potential. Moving on from the polarisations evident in much of the pioneer research in women's suffrage, this collection speculates on the complexities and apparent contradictions of the movement, an approach which succeeds in engaging the reader in the process, as queries mount and possibilities are rehearsed.

New research is evident within all these strands, and some essays incorporate many of the above themes. Chapters with a biographical focus covering Lily Maxwell, Mrs Henry Fawcett, Emmeline Pankhurst, Constance Lytton and Jennie Baines enable us to contrast famous with unknown activists, nudging us into re-evaluating our knowledge and understanding of a complex and diverse movement. The three 'famous' activists included here, Fawcett, Pankhurst and Lytton are, to some extent, blighted by their fame. In the face of their own extensive autobiographical writings and the expansive treatment by historians, feminist or otherwise, many might question how much there is left to discover about them. Inevitably, such doubt confirms that reappraisal provides novel interpretations as well as new material. Janet Howarth's work in 'Mrs Henry Fawcett (1847–1929): The widow as a problem in feminist biography', posits the question of 'the impact on her of Henry Fawcett's death, and the identity she created, or was encouraged to create, for herself as a political widow'(p.88). This is intriguing in the face of the common experience of Millicent Fawcett as an independent political activist, her brief marriage being subsumed within her long years of dedicated service to 'the Cause'. Like another famous activist widowed in youth, Charlotte Despard, we focus on their political endeavours and assume, as Howarth points out, that their widowhood was enabling, a premature freedom from the onerous duties of the Victorian married state. Marie Mulvey-Roberts, aware of the shock implicit in her title, 'Militancy, masochism or martyrdom? The public and private prisons of Constance Lytton', reassures the reader that her question is not meant to be heretical but seeks to, 'address the contradictions inherent within our understanding of victimhood and its paradoxical relationship to female empowerment' (p.159). Many of her controversial judgements about Lytton's personal life, however, such as her claim that her suffrage activism 'filled an emotional void….following an unhappy love affair' seem to be offered without sources. This alternative portrayal of one of the WSPU 'heroines', provides a significant opportunity to reflect on the confusions between an appreciation of an individual's political acts and the confines of biography. Is the inspiration we gain from Lytton's courageous acts impaired by a psychoanalytic portrait of the individual? Do we need such biographical information when what is of paramount concern is her campaigning and achievements? This is the issue which informs June Purvis's attempt to escape from the Pankhurst personality cult and concentrate on Pankhurst's political role in 'Emmeline Pankhurst (1858–1928) and Votes for Women' where she seeks to restore Pankhurst's obvious, yet often obscured, role in the political struggle for women's suffrage. Jane Rendall's 'Who was Lily Maxwell? Women's suffrage and Manchester politics, 1866–1867' and Judith Smart's, 'Jennie Baines: suffrage and an Australian connection' are witness to the increasing trend in suffrage history to broaden perspectives, establish links in terms of class and remind us of the international perspective of the suffrage struggle. To assuage immediate curiosity, Lily Maxwell actually voted in a Manchester by-election in 1868. However, this essay goes beyond biography by melding several important historiographical purposes in exposing the life of a working woman activist contextualised within the origins of women's suffrage and the wider suffrage debate whilst highlighting the regional significance of Manchester's role in the suffrage story.

The deficit in research into regional suffrage campaigning and organisations is further remedied with June Hannam's work in '"I had not been to London": Women's suffrage—a view from the regions'. Emphasising the incremental process of research which now enables this wider perspective to emerge, Hannam positions her research 'from the perspective of grassroots activism outside London and away from formal parliamentary politics' (p.227). Location dictates many differences in terms of vision, tactics and priorities, not only of great interest in themselves but also providing new questions with which to re-examine metropolitan suffrage research. '"Deeds, not words": Daily life in the Women's Social and Political Union in Edwardian Britain' also from Purvis provides some complementarity not only to her Pankhurst chapter, but also to other contributions which focus on previously 'unknown' activists and the pattern of their work for the Cause. In detailing the violence which many of the WSPU membership endured during the presentation of petitions and demonstrations, Purvis records that as part of rebuffing charges of being unnatural women, WSPU members were expected to preserve their decorous female behaviour, 'in all but militancy' (pp.137–8). Regarded as an army, one wonders if suffragettes were ever encouraged to fight back and employ self-defence when they were attacked? A revelation from Purvis is that force-feeding in prisons was also given to some women anally and vaginally. Although the sexual abuse of suffrage women during demonstrations has been well documented, this further example of state-sanctioned torture also warrants further research.

Hilary Frances's '"Dare to be free!": The Women's Freedom League and its legacy' and Alison Oram's, 'Women teachers and the suffrage campaign: Arguments for professional equality' both serve to elaborate on interpretive realignments and provide due weight to the activism of smaller organisations which nevertheless wielded significant influence. As a militant breakaway group from the WSPU, the democratic Women's Freedom League has not received the attention from scholars that the vigour and breadth of its pre-1914 campaigning deserve. Even less acknowledgement has been accorded to its stand 'to keep the suffrage flag flying' throughout the First World War and its subsequent essential role in mobilising the campaign for the final assault on women's franchise during the war. All this, plus its leadership during the 1920s struggle for the franchise extension whilst defending and extending women's rights, mark its significance. Within the confines of a single chapter, Frances provides a significant introduction to this fascinating group, exploring the complexities of its own attempts to do justice to the excitements of suffrage and emancipationist ideology. The strong links and multiple memberships between the National Union of Women Teachers and the Women's Freedom League is just one point of exploration as Oram unravels the conjunction between women teachers' claim for both suffrage and professional freedom. The way in which women teachers successfully transcended the seemingly obvious gender stereotyping involved in the connection between teaching and childcare, to elevate their position and establish themselves as professionals, gives credence to the value of women-only organisations. The ideological shift in campaigning strategies needed to fulfil all women's franchise claims, the contested fate of the women's movement and some of its chief protagonists, is the subject of the final chapter in this collection with Johanna Alberti's, '"A Symbol and a Key": The suffrage movement in Britain, 1918–1928'.

Contextualising the collection with historiographical and ideological assessments of this field of research are Sandra Stanley Holton's , 'The Making of Suffrage History' and 'The ideas of British suffragism' from Christine Bolt. That the ideology of the women's movement was varied, sophisticated in both argument and delivery, whilst sustaining ambitions beyond enfranchisement is Bolt's contention. She also sets the tone for the re-evaluative nature of this collection with her insistence that previous historians have not only neglected, but often ignored the work of women activists in Wales, Ireland and Scotland. One has only to study the maps of NUWSS and WSPU branch distribution (see Atkinson, 1988) to confirm the extent of suffrage branches beyond England. Holton's analysis of 'early models of suffrage history' crisply encapsulates her theme within four schools of such writing: constitutionalist, militant, masculinist and contemporary feminist. Her claim that 'analysing that achievement and placing it on record remain central to the project of feminist history' (p.29) confirms the contention that this is history on the move—the most exciting kind.

Cheryl Law
Birkbeck College

Taking a longer view of Nazism

Roderick Stackelberg, *Hitler's Germany: Origins, Interpretations, Legacies* (Routledge, London and New York, 1999) x+307pp., ISBN 0 41520 114 4 £15.99 pbk.

As Stackelberg explains in the introduction, *Hitler's Germany* was written to remedy the lack of a brief but comprehensive introductory text covering not only the Third Reich itself, but also the nineteenth-century background and the post-1945 legacies of Nazism. The book is aimed specifically at an undergraduate audience and is dedicated to the author's students at Gonzaga University, where he has taught a course on Hitler's Germany for over twenty years. Stackelberg has certainly identified a gap in the historiography, since other introductory studies of the Third Reich make few references to the period before 1918. Thirty years ago, Karl Dietrich Bracher's magisterial *The German Dictatorship* also dealt with the background and aftermath, but offered a much more comprehensive and ground-breaking analysis than the current author aims to provide.

Stackelberg begins with a clear outline of the interpretative approach that underpins the book. Nazism is defined as 'unambiguously a movement of the right', the most radical variant of fascism: counter-revolutionary in its hostility to the ideals of the Enlightenment and the French Revolution, and anti-modern in its blood and soil ideology, its anti-Semitism and its rejection of the emancipation of women. The author explains his differences with those historians, generally conservative or liberal-conservative, who place Nazism within the totalitarian tradition, closer to communism than to other movements of the right by virtue of its all-embracing ideology and ambition to control every aspect of the lives of its citizens. He also takes respectful issue with the late Detlev Peukert's emphasis on the 'modern' and technocratic aspects of Nazi rule and his view of National Socialism as the product of the crisis of modernity.

Chapters 2–5 of the book are devoted to the nineteenth- and early twentieth-century background and focus on those aspects of German history which the author sees as providing 'clues' to the eventual triumph of Nazism. There are sections, for example, on the failure of the 1848 revolutions, on the legacy of unification through Prussian military might, and on the emergence of expansionist and imperialist goals before 1914 at least partly to deflect pressures for domestic political reform. Particular attention is devoted to German ideology, an 'ultimately virulent combination of nationalism, racialism and moralism that formed part of the dominant secular belief system in Germany at the end of the nineteenth and the beginning of the twentieth centuries'. Stackelberg's analysis leans heavily on the *Sonderweg* thesis—the view that Germany's path to modernity was uniquely distorted until 1945 by its failure to develop a liberal constitutional structure to match the process of industrialisation and economic growth. Well aware of growing criticism of the thesis in recent years, the author is anxious to avoid any suggestion that he regards Nazism as the inevitable outcome of German historical development. Defeat in the First World War, the impact of the Russian Revolution, the political conflicts of Weimar and the effect of the Great Depression were, he emphasises, far more significant than any peculiarities of German history in explaining the triumph of Hitler. The section concludes with two chapters on the Weimar Republic and its fall which guide the reader skilfully through the conflicts of the period and include brief analysis of the Nazis' electoral appeal.

Stackelberg's survey of Hitler's Germany itself is presented in chapters 8–15. He offers a conventional account of the consolidation of the dictatorship in the early years of Nazi rule, and outlines the process of *Gleichschaltung* by which ordinary Germans were 'co-ordinated' into a national community from which racial, political and social 'undesirables' were ruthlessly excluded. Stackelberg is careful to show the importance not only of coercion but also of voluntary co-ordination from below, for example by professional associations of doctors and lawyers eager to adjust to the new realities. Domestic policy is further investigated with chapters on Nazi society and the persecution of the Jews before 1939. The focus then switches to foreign policy in the form of three chapters outlining the origins and the course of the Second World War. A well-written chapter on the Holocaust, containing an outline of developments and a brief summary of the historiographical debate between intentionalists and structuralists regarding the nature of the decision-making process and Hitler's role within it, completes the study of the Third Reich.

The short final section is devoted to the aftermath of National Socialism. After a summary of the denazification process and the emergence of two German states before 1950, it analyses the nature and extent of right-wing radicalism and anti-Semitism in the Federal Republic before and after reunification. The radical right is sensibly described as 'proportionately no larger than in other countries [but understandably giving] rise to greater international concern'. The author ends with a brief survey of the historiography of the Third Reich, predominantly in West Germany and the post-reunification Federal Republic. His remarks on the *Historikerstreit* of the 1980s offer judicious criticism of neo-conservative attempts to 'relativise' Nazism, and he has little sympathy for younger conservatives such as Rainer Zitelmann who emphasise the modernising and apparently left-wing aspects of Nazi rule. Stackelberg writes so clearly on the subject that one could have wished to see the section extended for the benefit of students new to the topic.

If the book has a significant weakness, it lies in the patchy treatment of Nazi society. There is very little on the role of women in the Third Reich despite the extensive literature on the topic, only half a page on education, and almost nothing on the attempt to indoctrinate an entire generation through the Hitler Youth. The German resistance also receives scant investigation, and even this is heavily weighted towards the military resistance at the expense of other aspects of defiance and nonconformity. Each of these topics receives less coverage than the German declaration of war on the United States, probably reflecting the fact that the book was written first and foremost for American students. Despite these caveats, the book is a useful concise introduction to the period and also contains an extensive English-language bibliography for each chapter for the guidance of readers seeking more detailed material.

Louise Willmot
Manchester Metropolitan University

The German Raj

Gerwin Strobl *The Germanic Isle. Nazi Perceptions of Britain* (Cambridge University Press, Cambridge, 2000), ISBN 0 52178 265 1, x+274pp., £25.00 hbk

It has long been accepted by historians that one of the Nazis' fundamental aims was to forge an 'alliance of equals' with 'Nordic' Britain and to emulate the ruthlessness of British rule in India by conquering and enslaving the 'inferior' Slavic races in Eastern Europe. Even though Hitler's view of Neville Chamberlain changed for the worse in the aftermath of the Munich crisis of October 1938, he continued to admire the English upper classes and their alleged instinct for self-preservation. During the war he falsely believed that Britain would eventually come to terms with a German-dominated Europe, if only to save its empire from ruin. Only in the final months of the war was he forced to recognise that he had been wrong in his assessment of the British people and their determination to fight to the bitter end.

Gerwin Strobl's book highlights all of these issues, but also goes beyond conventional treatments to examine the underlying assumptions behind Nazi attitudes towards Britain and the views and perceptions of 'ordinary' (i.e. middle-class) Germans during the inter-war period. Using a range of sources, including newspapers and weekly periodicals, as well as the diaries and political speeches of top Nazis, he shows that there was a surprising level of affection for Britain and British culture throughout the 1920s and 1930s. Memories of the British naval blockade and the wartime mood of *Gott strafe England* soon gave way to a notion that Britain was different from France, somehow more 'decent' and less bent on revenge against its erstwhile enemy. After the Ruhr crisis of 1923, for instance, the teaching of English in German schools became almost an act of patriotic defiance, and indeed it was during this period that English replaced French as the first foreign language for most educated Germans. Middle-class Germans in particular viewed England as a model of political stability and healthy national attitudes, as witnessed by the defeat of the General Strike in 1926, and the patriotic scenes during George V's Silver Jubilee in 1935 and George VI's Coronation in 1936. The sympathetic reporting of such events in the German press helped build popular support for Hitler's foreign policy in the 1930s; by this time, Britain appeared to most Germans, Nazi and non-Nazi alike, as a highly commendable country and a natural ally in the struggle against Bolshevism. Even the vigorous anti-British propaganda produced by Goebbels between 1939 and 1945 did nothing to dampen this enthusiasm for things English, which again found expression in the efforts of West Germans in the 1950s to rebuild links across the Channel.

One of the most interesting points which Strobl makes is how much of the Nazi image of Britain was based on ignorance. Hitler himself never visited Britain, nor could he speak English. His views were shaped by a number of unconventional sources, including the works of the racial anthropologist Hans Günther and the impressions of an assortment of travel writers whose portraits of the wider world were more amenable to him than the tortured prose of Foreign Office reports. Ordinary Germans too had little direct knowledge of Britain, especially as travel overseas was still a luxury beyond the means of most people. What little they did know tended to come from certain kinds of literature, in particular detective stories and the 'big names' like George Bernard Shaw and John Galsworthy. After 1933, independent sources on Britain were suppressed, while those stressing the supposed racial kinship with Germany were given extra prominence. This was acceptable to and even popular with ordinary Germans as long as it implied peace and stability in Europe.

Another interesting theme which Strobl develops concerns the use of language (and indeed it is no accident that one of his major sources is Viktor Klemperer's diaries). The words 'ruthless' and 'will' were among the most frequently used in the *lingua tertii imperii*, and were often applied to Britain. Thus for Hitler, writing in *Mein Kampf*, British wartime propaganda had been 'as ruthless as it was brilliant'. By contrast Wilhelmine Germany had not been ruthless enough to win the war; it had lacked Britain's will and determination to succeed. The lessons, to Hitler, were obvious. Only if Germany adopted similarly ruthless methods would Britain be prepared to accept her as an equal partner in world affairs, because only then would she have a realistic chance of winning wars in the future. Even at the height of the war Hitler returned to this theme. 'They [the British] are of incomparable impertinence, but I do admire them', he told Martin Bormann in August 1941.

Strobl's book is therefore a significant contribution to our understanding of the course of Anglo-German relations in the inter-war years, and in particular the complex and often contradictory attitude of Hitler towards the 'Germanic Isle'. However, one of the chief weaknesses of the book is the absence of a full and proper consideration of the question of continuity in German history, particularly the 'continuity of errors' in foreign policy between the First and Second World Wars. Admittedly this issue is no longer as significant in historiography as it was back in the 1960s and 1970s, when the Fischer controversy was still at its height. Nonetheless, the claim on the inside cover that the Nazis 'over-estimat[ed]… Britain's willingness to fall in with Germany and…under-estimat[ed]…Britain's determination to fight' surely has echoes of the 1897–1914 period.

The content of wartime Nazi anti-British propaganda was also scarcely original. Nearly all of the examples cited by Strobl were in fact imitations of propaganda produced in the 1914–18 period. Hence the idea of England as the 'land without music' goes back to a book published by the journalist Oskar Schmitz in 1914. Likewise British 'hypocrisy' and 'cant' were the themes of pamphlets published by (among others) Max Scheler and Houston Stewart Chamberlain in 1915. Anti-capitalist sentiments were also around during and after the First World War (see, for instance, Werner Sombart), as were the accusations that Britain was a 'betrayer' of the white race. Finally, Nazi propagandists owed an enormous debt to Count Ernst zu Reventlow, author of a virulent anti-British tract in 1915, *The Vampire of the Continent,* and of numerous anti-English articles in the right-wing newspaper the *Deutsche Tageszeitung*. Significantly Reventlow joined the Nazi party in 1927 and served as one of its Reichstag deputies until 1939. His best anti-English pieces were republished in two separate volumes by the Nazis in 1939–40. He receives only passing mention in Strobl's book, however.

The real value of Strobl's book lies in what it tells us about the hopes of ordinary Germans for an alliance with Britain in the 1930s, hopes which seem to have been genuine and sincere. The desire (which Hitler and the Nazis also shared, albeit for different reasons) was for acceptance by the

British as social equals. In this sense one of the most telling incidents in Anglo-German relations in the inter-war period took place during the Olympic games in Berlin in 1936. A group of British oarsmen were told by one of their German counterparts: 'If we weren't German, I think we should like to be British', to which they all replied with one voice that if they had not been born British, they would rather not have been born at all. As Strobl aptly puts it: 'Mutual incomprehension was thus complete'.

Mathew Stibbe
Liverpool Hope University College

National identity or class solidarity

Patrick Pasture and **John Verberckmoes** (eds), *Working-Class Internationalism and the Appeal of National Identity: Historical Debates and Current Perspectives on Western Europe* (Berg, Oxford, New York, 1998) ISBN 1 85973 28 1, 263pp., £44.95 hbk.

This volume edited by Patrick Pasture and John Verberckmoes, should be of particular interest to those in the field of labour and industrial relations. The broad approach of the book and treatment of the subject matter do have relevance for the general reader too, since the contributors address contemporary debates on various aspects of integration and harmonisation in European societies. The high price of the book however will not be an inducement for the general reader. The authors' foci on the roles and powers of trades unions within the context of the ongoing political, social, cultural and economic developments in western Europe merits serious attention. The book forms a useful basis to revisit some of the ideas on such subjects as class, internationalism, national identity, regionalism, Europeanisation of trades unions and solidarity. The main focus of this volume therefore is unions and workers, their affiliations and orientations within the context set by the authors.

The editors set out and explore contradictions in the thesis that 'working people have no country' and the reality of political and social nationalism as well as how the consequences of both can be same. An explicit message that emerges from this volume has implications in how class or workers solidarity is to be viewed. We may pose a question, which the authors seem to be asking, can we be citizens of the world, or in this case Europe, and who determines the contours and boundaries of such a citizenship, in which universalism, fraternalism, class solidarity of the workers and people have ascendancy? On the contrary internationalism and nationalism is conceptualised in relation to national and economic interests of the institutionalised systems that workers have to operate in. Working class as an identity marker and basis for affiliation may not prove to be as important or enduring a phenomenon as other markers such as, ethnic and religious affiliations or indeed economic interests of the workers and of course the unions! It would appear therefore that sectional interests assume a greater importance in manifestation, nature and level of internationalism for the workers and their unions. Thus a fundamental question arises about the nature of universalism and solidarity of the workers in practice.

The authors provide a contextual framework to the analysis and debates under discussion. In support of their contentions, the attitudes of the British working class are cited by the authors as examples of how class affiliation or more appropriately solidarity can be, both manipulated and subverted by considerations other than class itself. How for example the right in Britain exploited the working class during the 1960s and 1970s against non-white migrants and indeed the on-going attitudes towards the 'third world' migrants in Europe are proffered as testimony to what one can only be describe as parochialism of the unions and their members.

This state of affairs is quite evident in the contributions on union and workers' affiliation in two excellent pieces on Northern Ireland in the book by Norton and Helle respectively. Both cite religion as a more pronounced and salient marker of exclusivity than class solidarity, exemplified by the betrayal of what Norton calls 'true class interests' by the Protestant dominated unions. Perhaps Helle reflects the reality of broad sectional dimensions of all economic and industrial interest groups including the unions, when he says ' the question is no longer why socialism failed in Northern Ireland but how workers fitted in to Nationalism and Unionism.' How then Catholic and Protestant communities use these ideologies for their purposes is a more appropriate and apt analysis of the notion of solidarity than the more abstract universalism of the term 'workers of the world have no fatherland'. Put in another way, it could be translated to mean *why give up what you already possess?* The question of sharing, however is one which merits explanation in the Northern Ireland context. But for that the two chapters in the book referred to above are highly recommended. In the wider European context the book addresses the general lack of workers co-operation and joint action for common good.

The authors advocate European economic harmonisation and greater social and political integration, which would provide a structural basis for more formal and co-ordinated linkages of workers' organisations. Nevertheless the strengths of capital and the general economic conditions, coupled with political considerations in nation states, have a direct bearing on the level and nature of workers' cooperation and solidarity across national borders. In the climate of economic adversity self-interest becomes a dominant and powerful imperative for the workers to consider—the attitude of US workers to Japanese imports, and the fragmentation of unions and their members as a consequence of mass unemployment in Great Britain during the 1980s, are poignant examples. Arguably in the latter case, however, very little workers' solidarity could have been exercised even if the unions and their members had desired. The authors argue, quite rightly, that the unions and their leaders were not prepared to face the challenges and attitude of the Thatcherite state in Britain, and were 'content in preserving their patch'—hardly a recipe for concerted class action.

The authors address important issues facing European societies in general, and the working people and those who represent their interests in particular. These issues are addressed in the context of social, cultural and political conditions, which are increasingly determined by economic circumstances and the orientation of nation states in Western Europe. Quite rightly the authors address the concepts of workers' brotherhood in the diverse and plural settings of modern European societies. Thus a useful pointer is given for the reader to open up perspectives on class solidarity or identity affiliations, and the tendencies toward exclusivity borne of self-interest which the latter may denote. Yet, at the last, *Working-Class Internationalism and the Appeal of National Identity* would seem to be an attempt to recreate notions of equality and universal proletarian solidarity, leaving the authors to appear to be attempting to determine a new agenda on old certainties.

Zafar Khan is a writer on migration, settlement and identity

Historical memories and remembered histories

Raphael Samuel, *Island Stories: Unravelling Britain. Theatres of Memory*, Volume II, Verso, London, 1998, ISBN 1 85984 190 2, xxii+391pp., £13.00 pbk.

Island Stories: Unravelling Britain is the second volume of Raphael Samuel's collected writings, published under the title of *Theatres of Memory*. This volume is necessarily very different from the previous, *Theatres of Memory volume 1: Past and Present in Contemporary Culture*.[1] In Samuel's own words:

> The second volume—'Island Stories'—is about wildly different versions of the national past on offer at any given point in time, depending on whether the optic is that of the town or the country; centre or periphery; the state or civil society (ix).

The first volume was seen through to publication by Samuel himself. *Island Stories*, like future volumes, was put together by Alison Light, Sally Alexander and Gareth Stedman Jones. It comprises essays, not all of which were entirely finished, or rather, essays that had not been worked through to a final version. They all though have clear arguments, whether as rapid responses to contemporary situations or longer, thought-through enquiries simultaneously into past and present. Hopefully I can describe the complexion of the volume by way of the title. In the first part, the word stories, suggesting first that we are not to be offered final histories, authenticated and archived, but possible histories. Second, the word is *stories*, plural, both in the sense that, between these covers lies a range of topics, but also because narratives of pasts must necessarily be plural, if space is to be given to different voices. The second part of the title too indicates the argument. Unravelling, Samuel is intentionally unwinding the supposed wholeness, coherence, of these islands, deliberately replacing that unity with a diversity and difference that is better able to include accounts from varied experiences. At least that is how I put the unravelling going on here, although the reader should read the editors' comments on the word.

There are twenty-one essays, separated under five headings, the last of which is named 'Appendix'. The others are 'Nations, States and Empires', 'English Journeys', 'History, the Nation and the Schools' and 'The War of Ghosts'. The first group deal with issues of colonisation, inclusion or exclusion, identity and belonging. They range geographically from far to near, and question our sense of what the nation, this nation, is. I was particularly struck with the direct challenge to the idea that the islands—the British Isles— have a single history, or that their different histories add up to a coherent total. Rather there is the sense that what has made up the story of these islands is not finalised, not agreed, and open to interpretation. The unfinished nature of this story is caught by Samuel's departures into the contemporary political whirlpool, where the openness of the story, the future, is present in the essays own refusal to offer a single narrative, a closure.

The essays grouped under 'English Journeys' have a different tale to tell. In 'Country Visiting', where the text ends before completing what it has to say, Samuel recaptures pieces of childhood, growing up amid a radical family, for whom enabling the mind to think, required freeing the body to move. Country walking was a not a pasttime but a means of enhancing comradeship and dedication to a cause.

> For my mother…walking was a kind of religion, a secular form of uplift in which 'fresh air', 'exercise', and 'scenery' took the place of the Holy Trinity. (p.139)

The biographical insertion of 'Country Visiting' should not surprise the reader. Samuel is present in much that occurs between these covers. There is a sense of personal engagement with these stories. Of course, when necessary, Samuel is as able as any to provide the empirical details, the evidence—the copious footnotes that accompany several of these essays are evident of Samuel the archival historian, the academic. There is in fact an amusing account given by Alison Light in her biographical note of the manner of Samuel's indexing. Yet it is Samuel the remembrancer of our pasts that I take from this collection of essays. His refusal to set closure on those pasts, and his pulling together of different narratives, the accounts of the court historians of what our past has been, often presented in large volumes carrying the names of one or other ancient university, and the folk tale, the story passed on, elaborated and updated for our own times and purposes.

Contemporary political circumstance is rarely far away and at times it is these that take centre stage in the thrust of the essays. The struggle over school history, the National Curriculum, the GCSE syllabus, was probably the most important battle about history in recent years. The reason of course is obvious; what was taught through the school can be presented as the official history, it can be the only means for some children to learn their past, what has gone to make up the world they experience. Through the National Curriculum, who we are, our identity, could be influenced for good or ill. History Workshop, with Raphael Samuel, engaged in that debate in attempts to forge a history that was not closed—only one, official, account being privileged, and inclusive—being part of these islands, or the nation, was not dependent on place of origin or status of residence. The essays under 'History, the Nation and the Schools' were engagements in that debate, being originally published in national newspapers or in one case, *London Review of Books*. In each case they sought to intervene in a debate on a then Conservative Party initiative for history teaching in schools, the consequences of which would have been at best disastrous.

The sense of the present reccurs in the next set of essays, 'The War of Ghosts'. The essays range wonderfully among the great historian R.H. Tawney, Puritanism, the Tory Party at Prayer, and the attempt by Margaret Thatcher to repossess/reprocess Victorian values to substantiate her version of society. The movement back and forth in these essays is some of the most potent in the book. There is a real diversity of nature and style of essay in the section. 'Religion and Politics: The Legacy of R.H. Tawney', which started life as a letter to the *Guardian*, and then grew and grew and grew. Similarly 'The SDP and the New Middle Class' started life as a piece for *New Society*. 'Ancestor Worship' is remarkable for its brevity, fewer than three pages. In each, the argument of the essay is left to stand on its own, their nature as interventions seemingly precluding the addition of notes. 'The Discovery of Puritanism, 1820–1914: A preliminary sketch', and 'Mrs Thatcher and Victorian Values' are, despite the first title, worked through, and supported by copious notes with references in the style of conventional historical writing. It is this variation of style and purpose that makes *Island Stories* so readable, and often enjoyable. The reader proceeds from immediate interventions in a contemporary political matter, to a conventional academic essay.

To sum up a volume like this is pointless. Perhaps that is how it should be. I shall avoid the task by giving the last words to Alison Light, Sally Alexander and Gareth Stedman Jones:

> Never satisfied with the assertions of official knowledge or the protocols of academic or political orthodoxy, Raphael Samuel looked for the tensions in an argument and deepened them. (xi)

Note

1. See Victor Kiernan 'History Manicured?', *Socialist History* 8, 1995.

Stephen Woodhams
Birkbeck College

Socialist History Journal

The *Socialist History Journal* explores and assesses the past of the socialist movement and broader processes in relation to it, not only for the sake of historical understanding, but as an input and contribution to the movement's future development. The journal is not exclusive and welcomes argument and debate from all viewpoints.

Other *Socialist History* titles

A Bourgeois Revolution?
Socialist History 1 · 1993
0 7453 0805 8

What Was Communism? Pt 1
Socialist History 2 · 1993
0 7453 0806 6

What Was Communism? Pt 2
Socialist History 3 · 1993
0 7453 08074 1

The Labour Party Since 1945
Socialist History 4 · 1994
0 7453 0808 2

The Left and Culture
Socialist History 5 · 1994
0 7453 0809 0

The Personal and the Political
Socialist History 6 · 1994
0 7453 0810 4

Fighting the Good Fight?
Socialist History 7 · 1995
0 7453 1061 3

Historiography and the British Marxist Historians
Socialist History 8 · 1995
0 7453 0812 0

Labour Movements
Socialist History 9 · 1996
0 7453 0813 9

Revisions?
Socialist History 10 · 1996
0 7453 0814 7

The Cold War
Socialist History 11 · 1997
0 7453 1241 1

Nationalism and Communist Party History
Socialist History 12 · 1997
0 7453 1267 5

Imperialism and Internationalism
Socialist History 13 · 1998
1 85489 107 3

The Future of History
Socialist History 14 · 1998
1 85489 109 X

Visions of the Future
Socialist History 15 · 1999
1 85489 115 4

America and the Left
Socialist History 16 · 1999
1 85489 117 0

International and Comparative Labour History
Socialist History 17 · 2000
1 85489 119 7

Cultures and Politics
Socialist History 18 · 2000
1 85489 123 5

Life Histories
Socialist History 19 · 2001
1 85489 129 4